I0142347

THE KING
OF
PACOIMA

DAVID MICKEY EVANS

FLYING WAGON BOOKS, LLC

FLYINGWAGONBOOKS@GMAIL.COM
HTTPS://WWW.FACEBOOK.COM/PAGES/FLYING-WAGON-
BOOKS/489699814379554

Flying Wagon Books
New Smyrna Beach, Florida
FlyingWagonBooks@Gmail.com
https://www.facebook.com/pages/Flying-Wagon-Books/
489699814379554

Copyright July, 2012 by David Mickey Evans. All Rights
Reserved.
http://www.davidmickeyevansblog.blogspot.com

No part of this book may be used or reproduced, stored in a
retrieval system, or transmitted by any means in any manner
whatsoever without the written permission of the author. For
information about permission to reproduce selections from this
book, contact David Mickey Evans at
FlyingWagonBooks@Gmail.com

First Edition, 2014

ISBN # 978-0-9915999-0-5 (paperback)
E-ISBN # 978-0-9915999-1-2 (e-book)
U.S. Copyright Registration Number: TXu 1-820-064
Library of Congress Control Number: 2014916290
Flying Wagon Books, New Smryna Beach, Florida

Printed in the United States of America

Book Cover photograph by Jane Linders
Cover design by Stacey McGillis
Illustrations by Arlan Jewell
Storyboards by Paul Power
Photographs by permission from David Mickey Evans
Photo blur by Steiner Creative, Los Angeles
Image manipulation and composites by Stacey McGillis
Format and layout by David Mickey Evans

For
Ray Bradbury,
whose books saved my life growing up.
and
G, G, O & H.
and
The child in everyone.

Wide, wide in the Rose's side
Sleeps a child without sin
And any man who loves in this world
Stands there on guard over him.
- Kenneth Patchen,
When we were here together

"But Dad, they're made of wax."
- Icarus

"And what are we supposed to
fill it with, hot air?"
- Joseph Mongolfier

"Good luck, brother."
- Wilbur Wright

CONTENTS

Mike and Bobby. 1966.

1

VALIANT PEANUT BUTTER

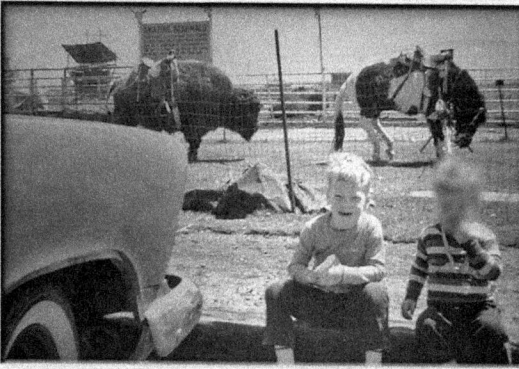

COLOR
TRANSPARENCY

MADE IN THE U.S.A

"For God speaks again and again, in dreams,
in visions of the night when deep sleep falls
on men as they lie on their beds."
- Job 33:15

This is what I remember:

The vinyl covered back seat of a five-year-old 1961 Plymouth Valiant. Hours and hours over an endless stretch of blacktop whose dashed divider line was faded from long, hot midwest summers.

Somewhere in the Oklahoma panhandle.

A Buffalo farm.

A small town we went through on our way there.

A town that had grown up a stone's throw from the Buffalo farm after the Federal highway system had spread like the lines of a cracked windshield through the very places the Buffalo used to roam.

The highway brought tourists in dark socks and bright shirts with Kodak instamatic cameras who took pictures of the last of America's last great beasts.

The town had a shop-lined street with a swirling red and white barber's pole; an ice cream parlor with a spotless chrome soda fountain; a helpful hardware store where everybody in the town had a tab; a sweet smelling tobacco shop with a wooden Indian standing guard outside; a post office with brass clerk's cages and an old Post Master who always smiled at you when you went in to pick up a package from the Sears catalogue that was too big to fit in your mailbox. A package that may have come from way back east, where we had come from.

All the people who lived there were perfect people, the type who used any excuse for a parade down main street. Like Friday football games at the high school when all the local sons suited up for the grid iron; a watermelon festival in August; a going away parade for the neighborhood girl who was accepted to college, and always, of course, a Veterans of Foreign Wars parade, when all of the old timers would walk - wheeling their buddies who couldn't - past misty-eyed relatives who saluted them with as much respect as they'd been given when they stepped off the boat back to their families after the big war many years before.

No one there ever got mad at anyone else. There were never any arguments. Never any fights, and when Mr. Smith would have too much to drink at the town's one tolerated saloon, Sheriff Andy would let him sleep it off in an unlocked jail cell and bring him hot coffee and aspirin in the morning.

COLOR
TRANSPARENCY

MADE IN THE U.S.A

When anyone moved into town, the local Ladies Auxiliary would deliver enough homemade Welcome-to-our-Town food that the new family wouldn't have to go to Honest Bob's Grocery Store for a month.

Every family in town had a house. All with red brick chimneys and big front porches that made them all match like the tiny accessory-houses in a fairy tale town through which a Lionel H.O. scale Pride O' Topeka model railroad would run. But at the same time they were all different, each one with its particular family's spirit surrounding it. Some had porch swings, others two chairs and a table; some tidy flower beds, others trim green lawns; some maple trees, others oaks; some with children in the front yard safe within their white picket fences, others with elderly people waving warmly from their porches to passersby. It wasn't the similarities but the little familial differences that made each house as homey and warm and wonderful as the one next door. As families grew, carpenter and plumber and electrician friends of the father would all show up one day unannounced, and help build on an extra room for the price of a meatloaf sandwich and lemonade lunch, and the knowledge that when their families grew they would get the same in return.

Even though I was four years-old, I'm sure that I was right when I figured that no one there in the most perfect small town in America had any idea what an apartment was.

Bobby and me and our Mom were going to Los Angeles. We were going to live in an apartment.

As we passed through the small town and continued out toward the Buffalo farm, Mom told us that we were in Oklahoma, and that so far we had traveled one thousand five hundred miles. Miles didn't mean anything to Bobby and me because we didn't know what they were, but peanut butter jars did. So by the time we got to the Buffalo farm in Oklahoma we were seven empty jars away from

Pennsylvania.

Bobby was two years-old and because the back seat of the Valiant was crowded with all our toys and Mom's stuff, he had to climb over me to look out the window to try and see the Buffalo.

Only a few scattered stones were left in the parking lot from the gravel that had once covered it. The rocks had mostly all been carried away down the slope of the road by rainwater, leaving only dirt. Clouds of the lot-dirt dusted the windows so we couldn't see the Buffalos too well when we first pulled up.

Mom parked us by the souvenir stand. When we got out, Bobby and I came face-to-face with an old whiskey barrel. We stood staring at it with our mouths open. Except for the giant Dinosaur in Missouri that they had turned into a hamburger stand when it died, the barrel was about the greatest thing we had ever seen. Not the barrel itself, but what was in the barrel. It was open on the top and held real live, authentic, Genuine American Indian rubber-tipped bamboo spears. The sign on the barrel told us so, it said, "Genuine American Indian Spears: 50 cents."

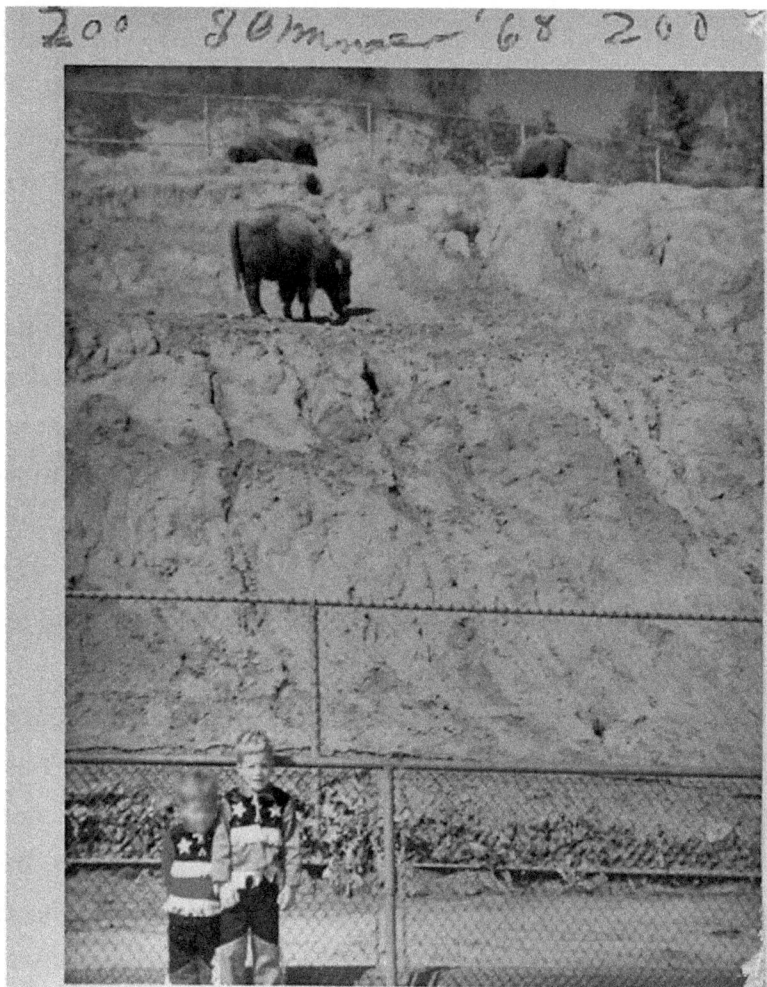

Bobby and Mike. Full dress cowboy outfits. 1968.

Even though Bobby and me were young, we knew how important money was. After fifteen hundred miles, when still the novelty of traveling across the country hadn't worn off (we were never easily bored), we knew enough to know that what was happening was serious business. We'd never asked Mom why our Dad hadn't come with us or why we were going to Los Angeles to live in an apartment where Mom was going to have to pay rent, but we knew that rent meant money and that Mom didn't have too much of it. Since we understood all of this, it was no big deal that most of the neat things we saw we couldn't have. We didn't feel bad about it, we adapted. We developed the ability to store the look and feel of neat things like the Genuine Indian Spears away in our heads, so that any time we wanted to we could call up those memories and pretend those things were ours for a while. Most times our recalled imaginings were better than the real thing because we never had put the toy away after we played with it.

Mom always told us we were the best sons she could've asked for because we didn't ask for anything. We didn't ask because it made Mom sad when she couldn't get us neat things we wanted, so imaginings were just fine with us. But of all the neat stuff we'd seen from Pennsylvania to Oklahoma, the Genuine American Indian rubber-tipped bamboo spears were the greatest. Possessing them only through an imagining was almost impossible.

I stood there holding Bobby's hand so he wouldn't wander off and Mom probably saw us staring at the barrel because, except for an old man in a cowboy outfit with a long grey beard, we were the only people visiting the Buffalo farm that day.

"Hi boys, welcome to the Geronimo Bill Buffalo Farm."

"Hi."

"Hi."

Mom came around the car and I pulled Bobby away from the barrel hoping she wouldn't see us staring at the spears. The sign at the entrance said, "Admission - 25 cents."

"Afternoon Ma'am, couple a fine lookin' boys ya got there."

"I'm sorry, but would it be okay if I just set them on the fence so they could see the Buffalo?"

COLOR TRANSPARENCY

MADE IN THE U.S.A

I knew why Mom asked him that. I felt sorry for her because she usually said things like that at places she couldn't afford to buy us into. Geronimo Bill didn't answer at first. He looked down at me and Bobby, and we had our matching cowboy outfits on that day, and then over to his parking lot where there weren't any cars except for ours.

"Well Ma'am," Geronimo Bill said, "this is your lucky day. It's free admission day for folks from out of town." He opened the gate and let us in, "So, you go on in and stay to the trail and enjoy yourselves."

Mom said thank you and took my hand and I held Bobby's and we went through the turnstile. As we went through I looked at the little numbers that tell how many people have been there. It read: 00015. The dial was really old and dusty so I knew that only 15 people had visited the Buffalo farm in long, long time... I knew Geronimo Bill didn't make much money, but he felt sorry for Mom too. Geronimo Bill was a very nice old man.

"Okay you guys, don't get scared, the Buffalos are behind a fence." Mom told us as we got closer to the viewing area.

"Mom, Buffalos don't eat people, they eat grizzly bears and stuff." I set Mom straight about the relative safety of Buffalo viewing - in the time it had taken us to walk from the gate to the viewing area, I had become an expert on the beasts. Bobby on the other hand kept tip-toeing to peek through the old fence boards to be sure there were no surprises. Then, without looking at us, Mom smiled so I knew she was just kidding.

When we got to the brick steps that you stood on to see over the fence, there was a sad kind of surprise. Far away in the middle of a plain dirt field with some old truck tires with hay in them and an old bathtub full of water, were the last of the Great American Bison.

They didn't walk around much; just sort of stood in the middle of the little corral and swatted at the flies with their tails. They didn't make any noises. They didn't stampede like the Buffalos on the big posters nailed to the fence. There weren't great herds of them like there were on the postcards in the souvenir shop. There were only three Buffalos at the farm; a Big One with horns and two small ones with their horns broken off.

Bobby stared and stared at them, inching farther up the fence until Mom set him on top of it. I could see fine, so I stood on the steps, and although I didn't know why, I felt sadder than I ever had before. Their fur was old and dirty and falling off; they looked very, very old. After a minute the Big One looked over, and I swear, because I remember this most of all, that he looked right at me and there were tears in his big brown eyes. I know it's true because Mom picked up Bobby and took me by the hand and said, "Come on guys, we don't want to disturb them too much."

At the entrance Mom said thank you again to Geronimo Bill. He tipped his hat and looked like, in his heart, he knew that the Buffalos cried all the time, but that he didn't know where else to take them.

We got in the car and just before Mom pulled away, Geronimo Bill came over and waved her to stop. She rolled the window down and he leaned in and said, "Good luck to you, Ma'am." He tipped his hat again, stepped back from the car and then suddenly remembered something very important.

"Oh, almost forgot, here you go boys, take care of yer Ma now, ya hear?" With that, Geronimo Bill handed Bobby and me each a brand new, Genuine American Indian rubber-tipped bamboo spear. Free of charge.

As we drove away, Mom watched the road ahead, and Bobby and me, holding our Genuine Indian Spears, watched out the back window. Through the dust we could see Geronimo Bill go into the corral. Just before he got too far away to see anymore, we saw him feed the Buffalos some hay by hand and pet the Big One on the back like an old, old friend.

COLOR
TRANSPARENCY

MADE IN THE U.S.A

The highway we were on was long and straight and at the end of it, where the road met the sky, the sun was sinking down like a big orange ball about to be lost forever behind a neighbor's backyard fence.

Just as the sun disappeared for that day, and the night and stars came across the sky, my memory fades. I remember only fragments for sometime after that.

A Howard Johnson's, in Tulsa, Oklahoma.

A Holiday Inn, in Albuquerque, New Mexico.

A Best Western, in Phoenix, Arizona.

A KOA campground with a pool in Mojave, California where we slept in the car because, even though she didn't tell us, Mom was running out of money.

Finally, after fifteen jars of peanut butter, over big roads, little streets, through small towns like in Oklahoma, big cities like in Ohio, lots of gas stations, through mountains where the Valiant smoked and coughed and sometimes stopped running and Mom let it rest, by lakes with boats on them, cold places and deserts we arrived at a second floor apartment in Los Angeles, above an Aunt we didn't even know we had.

A few years go by before I can recall anymore. And then, a man who was a friend of our Aunt's husband.

A man who seemed very nice.

One day he wore a nice suit and a sharp tie and silver cufflinks you could see yourself in.

Me and Bobby got shiny new shoes, new shirts and clip-on ties and haircuts and we looked pretty spiffy.

Mom got a new dress.

COLOR
TRANSPARENCY

MADE IN THE U.S.A

A court house.

We got to throw rice.

And then he was our new Dad.

Disneyland.

A new, bigger apartment.

Our own room.

Christmas when Bobby was five and I was seven.

Bunk beds. New bikes.

G.I. Joe flashlights and walkie-talkies from Grandma

and Pop-Pop back east.

A red Radio Flyer wagon.

A movie called "Born Free" and Mom cried when she watched it.

A baby sister.

Nights that lasted a long time because there was screaming.

Our baby sister never cried, she wasn't screaming.

Darkness.

And then I remember more...

The only thing I could see when I would look up on those nights was the bottom springs of the top bunk bed. Bobby and I played a game of Yahtzee for dibs on the top bed and he lost. But I knew he wanted the top one, so I told him since I won I'd take the bottom.

On all the endless nights I could never get to sleep I would hide inside my Coleman Map-of-America sleeping bag with the zipper up the side that never worked. I would imagine being in all the places on the map, faded from too many washings, while Bobby constantly shifted and wrestled in his sleep above me. There was a picture of a big Buffalo on the inside of the sleeping bag and it was standing in the middle of an endless field of yellow grass. I imagined it was the Big One, the one that Geronimo Bill knew cried in the plain dirt corral. I would reach underneath my bed to where I hid my Genuine American Indian Spear in case of sneak attack, and hold onto it, and stare at the map in my sleeping bag and watch an imaginary movie of the time we stopped in Oklahoma.

The shouting and screaming went on.

Bobby always fell asleep faster than me.

Not too long after we moved into the new apartment some things started happening to him. When he slept, he rolled all over the place like a fish when you pull it out of the water. Some nights he would be still for a long time and others he thrashed around for hours.

I guessed he was having bad dreams, which he was, because he told me so when I asked him. But when I asked him what the dreams were about he would never tell me. He just always said, "They were nightmares."

And they got worse.

BUFFALO GETS
BIGGER, RUNS FASTER
WE PUSH INTO ANIMATED VIEW

BUFFALO IN

THE STATE EXPANDS OUT AS
WHEAT FIELDS GROW.

MIKE: "I HAVE TO, MY BROTHER'S HAVING A NIGHTMARE"

BUFFALO! "WHEN YOU NEED ME... I'LL BE THERE!"

One night, very late, Bobby and me got all the way inside our sleeping bags with our flashlights and walkie-talkies and turned the volumes down so only we could hear.

"Aren't ya gonna tell me what the dreams are?" I whispered, communicating via walkie-talkie.

"No. They're just nightmares, but too scary." His voice crackled back.

"Well, maybe if you tell me then they won't be scary anymore." I reasoned.

"No, they will. It don't matter." He said.

"How do you know?" I asked.

"Just 'cause. Besides I don't remember 'em after I wake up, only that they're scary."

I had a plan. "Okay, when you have another one and I see you rolling around, I'll wake you up and you can tell me what it was."

He thought about this for a minute. "I dunno, Mike, you might tell Mom." We hadn't told her that Bobby had nightmares. "And I don't wanna tell her, 'cause she might tell The King and he might get mad at me."

"No, I won't tell her. Here…" I held my left pinkie up toward the top bunk bed, "Pinkie promise, I swear I won't tell her if you tell me."

Bobby locked pinkies with me. We made an oath that the next time he had a nightmare I would wake him up and he would tell me what it was about.

We turned off our walkie talkies and doused the flashlights, and Bobby went to sleep. I stayed up and watched and waited.

There was some screaming and shouting that night that stopped after a while.

I tried to stay awake, but my eyes wouldn't do what I told them to and they closed.

Darkness.

I did not dream that night.

It started to rain in our room.

I felt it in my sleep and woke up after I was all wet.

For a minute after my eyes opened I thought I was outside. Then when I looked up at the springs beneath the top bunk bed, I saw they were soaked. And they were squeaking.

Bobby and Mike. Good boys. 1969.

Bobby was bouncing all over the place.

He was having a nightmare.

It was the scariest one he had ever had.

Bobby had wet his bed.

And he had never, ever, peed his pants before.

I got out of bed and reached up to shake Bobby awake. He was turned away from me and it was then for the first time that I saw the bruises on his back.

He sat up real fast and stared at me for a long time before he was fully awake. Then closed his eyes again like he was trying to hide from a monster.

"What was it? What was the nightmare about?" I whispered before he could forget.

When his eyes opened, there were tears in them.

"Bobby, come on, what was the nightmare about?" I asked again.

He didn't want to tell me, but he did, real slow.

"The King..." he said, "The King was chasing me and I couldn't get away."

Bobby. A worried buckaroo. 1969.

2

THE VALLEY OF DREAMS

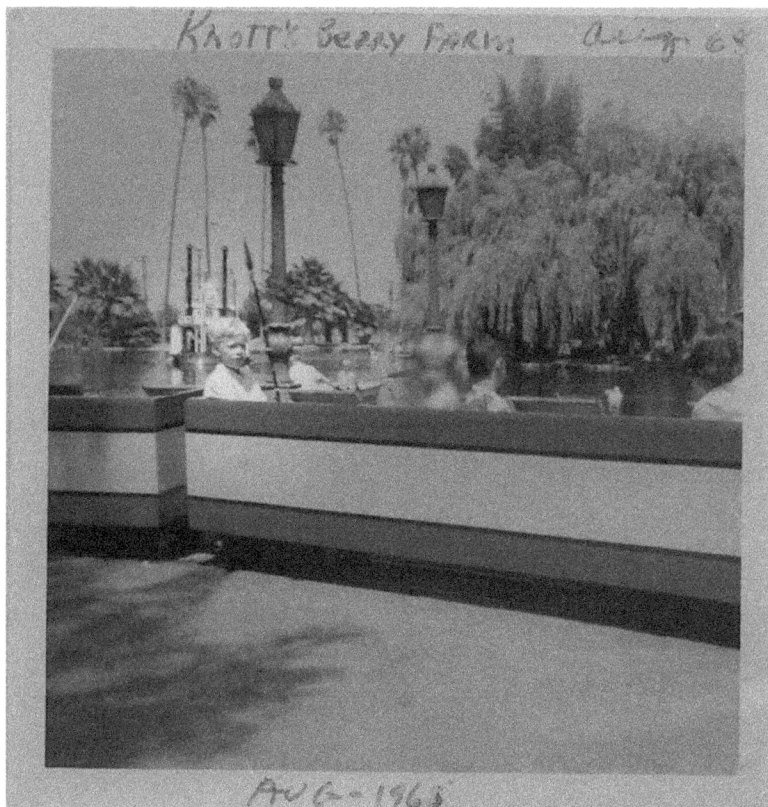

Knott's Berry Farm   aug 64

Aug - 1968

*"To all who come to this happy place, Welcome...
Here youth may savor the challenge and promise of the
future..."*
- Walt Disney, Disneyland Dedication Plaque

A little while after we first came to California and after

Mom didn't look sad too often anymore and things were pretty happy and good, we got to go to Disneyland.

I remember the very second we walked through the gates and onto Main Street U.S.A. Bobby and me felt like we belonged there because the whole place looked like all the small towns with perfect houses and shops we had seen three years before when Mom drove us across America.

We wanted to live there in one of the little houses that had a candy shop on the ground floor and stairs that went up toward a brick chimney that looked exactly like all the chimneys on the houses in the small town near the Buffalo farm in Oklahoma. We didn't ever want to leave Disneyland, but when we did we made a pretty good haul. Bobby got a Davy Crocket coon skin cap and I got a special map of Disneyland, which to Bobby and me was a map of the whole world. It wasn't too long after we went to Disneyland, in the summer when Bobby was eight and I was ten, that we moved.

Mike, Bobby, Mom and Grandma.
The Happiest Place on Earth. 1967.

In the middle of the hottest month in the middle 1968, we moved a million miles away. Mom told us that is was only about thirty miles from our apartment, but we went back and forth so many times from our apartment to the new place while we were moving, that if you added up the number of peanut butter jars it would've taken to make all those trips, it would've been about a hundred.

Moving was no big deal because not only had Mom and Bobby and me moved three times before, we had driven all the way across America to do it. So we were pretty much experts on moving by then. But it wasn't so much where we were moving that was important, it was what we were moving into that made Mom seem real happy.

Since we had been living in city apartments - or when we lived in Pennsylvania, with relatives in houses on crowded streets - a tract house in a real neighborhood with real trees and all that, was a dream come true for her. For Bobby and me, since we had had a big taste of what exploring was like when we traveled across the country, the east San Fernando Valley was a place of boundless suburban wonder. We never dreamed that we would get to live in a place where we could explore more than just the halls of an apartment building.

The backyard of our new house.
Suburban wonderland. 1969.

The house we got had a big backyard with a redwood fence and a matching redwood clubhouse that was built out of the scrap. The fence boards were dry and cracked and loose on their nails. Bobby and I noticed this right away (eight and ten-year-olds notice things like loose nails), and it seemed important so we didn't tell anybody about the loose boards. The clubhouse was spar-varnished to protect it against the rain, but that summer was really hot, and the heat made the whole thing bleed sap like an axed maple tree. Across the backyard, next to the north fence, was a brick barbecue with redwood cupboards and across from that, along the north side of the house, we even had a place to keep garbage cans.

The first place that attracted us like two moths to a spotlight was the field behind the east fence. It stretched down the entire block behind all the houses in the tract.

After we had helped move the last load of stuff out of the truck and into the house, we found the loose fence boards and squeezed through into the east field. There was so much incredible stuff back there that at first we just stood staring into the suburban wilds thinking the same thoughts we had had when we'd first seen the barrel of Genuine American Indian Spears at the Buffalo farm. It was almost too much to take.

There were peach trees with peaches as big as softballs, eight foot sunflowers with flower parts as big as frisbees, mounds of gravel with stones the absolute perfect size for slingshots, a stack of really old wooden pallets that were covered in creosote and grown over by the sunflowers, about a million kinds of sun-bleached play balls that had bounced over backyard fences and were left to weather and rot (we collected all these, of course), and an old construction shack with a rusty lock on the door.

Now of all of the things there were to explore and discover in the field, of all the time we would have for the rest of our lives to wander through the field and hunt down imaginary enemies, of all the stuff there was to collect, look at, test, try out, mess around with... the first thing we did was try the lock on that door. It wouldn't budge.

The windows of the shack were greasy and dark.

I boosted Bobby up on my shoulders to window level for a general monster and bogeyman check. He wiped a spot clear on the window with his sleeve and squinted inside with his hands cupped around his eyes.

"No, no bad guys."

"What's in there?" I asked

Bobby squinted harder. "Umm... Hey! There's a engine in there, like from a grass cutter thing."

"Bobby... Mike?" We heard Mom calling us from the new house, so we filed the location of the engine away for future reference and headed back across the tall grass to the loose boards in the fence.

A couple of days went by before all of mom's stuff and all of His stuff was arranged in the house so that it looked like a house and not an apartment. It had only taken Bobby and me about ten minutes to stash all of our stuff in our room. We couldn't understand why they didn't just shove all their stuff in their closet like we did with ours. Bobby and me only had to open our closet door and there it was. Clothes. Games. Slingshots. School stuff. Couple of half eaten tuna sandwiches. Lunch boxes. Shoes. All of it fit in there perfectly and our room was never messy.

After the house turned into what Mom called a home, we were freed from the toil of straightening and arranging and moving and putting away. We never understood why stuff always had to be straight and neat and put away. What was the point? It was all gonna get messed up again anyway. But, it made Mom happy when things were nice, so we did it. And then we had some serious exploring time to make up for.

In the days that followed, Bobby and me explored every square inch of everywhere from our house to a certain place where we ended up spending a lot of time.

We didn't know it was there, we just happened upon it on one of our expeditions. From the corner it was just a little drive-thru Jessup dairy, which we could tell had been there for a long time because it had old tin advertisement signs for cigarettes that looked exactly like the ones we had seen on old drive-thru markets in other states where Mom had bought peanut butter and crackers on our trip from Pennsylvania.

The first time we explored near the drive-thru we had no idea what was behind it.

That day, Bobby and me had 28 cents between us, so we bought two cheese n' crackers and two wax bottle cokes; the kind in the bottle you could chew after you drank the coke, and spit out the wax after you sucked all the juice out of it. And since great stuff like that was dirt-cheap back then, we still had 8 cents left. We sat down on the curb and it wasn't too long before we heard it.

Moo…

We turned around slow and saw where the dairy got its milk from. More cows than we had ever seen, even more than on the farms we had passed in the middle of America.

Everywhere we explored we took our Genuine American Indian Spears with us in case of sneak attack. When we would go to the dairy and stand outside the fence and look at the big black and white cows, we would hold on to the spears real tight and imagine and remember and wish to go back to the Geronimo Bill Buffalo Farm and say hello to the two little ones with the broken horns and the Big One with the tears in his eyes.

About 100 miles - six blocks - from the dairy there was a

place surrounded by a fence with a sign that warned, "Power Company Land--No Trespassing!" But when Bobby and me read it, it said, "Free Explorations--COME ON IN!" We learned later that everyone called it The 500, because it was five hundred acres of land. This land was different than the other land around the area; it was sandy and dusty and almost like the deserts in New Mexico and Arizona. It had giant drainage pipes which you could hike up inside for hundreds of yards into the pitch black darkness until you got so scared you turned around and ran all the way back out.

There were strange noises in those pipes.

Squeaks.

Millions of squeaks.

We only went to The 500 drainage pipes when we needed a dangerous expedition.

We didn't go too often.

We found frogs in the water of those pipes.

Big frogs.

Millions of frogs.

Later on, after a certain expedition, on a certain day, Bobby and me never, ever explored the pipes at The 500 again.

So for the most part we explored the field behind our fence. It was big enough and jammed with enough stuff to devote days of scouting to. After we knew every single patch of dirt and had looked under every rock in that field, we ventured beyond it. We explored in the opposite direction, away from our backyard fence with the loose boards.

Beyond that field, across San Fernando Road - the oldest street in the area - were train tracks that were so long, and so straight, that when you stood on the corner of Osborne Blvd., where it crossed San Fernando Road, you could not see the end of them. In fact, we reasoned they went all the way to China. As it turned out, they went even further.

One day we followed the tracks for hours. The tracks weren't exactly straight like we first thought. We got to the end of the straight part and they curved easily left and disappeared behind a giant mountain of rocks. There, instead of following the tracks, we climbed up the mountain. At the top, when we looked back in the direction we'd come from, it turned out to be an empty county reservoir. The rock mountain wasn't a mountain at all, but a dam that hadn't held back any water in a long time. When we looked forward, over the dam, we saw rolling hills and lots of trees. It was very strange; on one side of the rocks it was like a desert and on the other it was beautiful and lush and green. We started carefully down the mountain toward the green hills that stretched out like a gigantic backyard as far as we could see. When we got to the bottom we stepped off the rocks and onto a small dirt path. There were tire tracks in the dirt.

Beep! Honk! Bobby and I jumped across the little road and rolled down a hill into a pile of fresh mowed grass on the other side of the path. We'd almost been run over by two men in a little car that hardly made any noise when it moved, so we hadn't heard it coming. It was a golf cart. The gigantic backyard we had seen from the top of the rock mountain was a golf course.

Mike, Bobby and our Little Sister in the Radio Flyer. 1970.

We sat there for a minute until the golf cart disappeared around another hill and we were sure that it was gone and wasn't coming back. We had never seen a golf course before, but we figured that if they were all this big there couldn't be very many of them, otherwise they'd take up the whole world. Through the trees, standing near flags on really flat green spots, we could see nicely dressed people. Since they were all adults we suspected that we probably shouldn't be there. But the place was too good not to explore. So we did.

We made our way across the golf course and almost got hit by a couple of flying golf balls. There were lots of golf balls all over the place; wedged in the limbs of trees, half-buried in little sand pits, under rocks and even in the bottoms of shallow ponds where ducks might eat them. Every time we saw a golf ball fall in the water, or roll up a hill, or bounce into the rocks of the mountain we heard far away voices yelling bad words very loudly. We guessed the golf balls weren't supposed to be going into those places. We guessed no one would go after them. We guessed that they considered them lost. And because the golfers all cursed when it happened, we guessed that golf balls cost money.

We guessed right.

We came to this small place - like a house in the middle of the golf course - with a sign that read, "Pro Shop." Golfers would go in with their wallets and come out with golf balls. After we'd watched this happen five or six times an idea started to grow in my head.

"Hey Bobby, what if we collected all the golf balls that go up the hill and stuff?"

"Yeah, so what?" Bobby didn't get it yet.

"There must be a million balls out there. So if we go get 'em, maybe we could make 'em buy 'em back." I reasoned.

Bobby caught on real fast. "Okay."

We got two paper bags out of the trash and started hunting for golf balls. It only took about an hour to fill both bags to the top with balls. We went back to the Pro Shop and stood outside. Our idea was that when anybody started into the Pro Shop with their wallets out, we would ask if they wanted to buy the golf balls we had instead of the new ones in the little boxes.

One man, the first golfer that came by, bought them all.

He gave us five dollars.

We could absolutely not believe he gave us five dollars. All we gave him was a hundred and twenty seven lousy golf balls and he gave us five dollars. As Bobby and me passed the bill back and forth staring at it, feeling it, snapping it open and closed, a feeling came over us. We both felt it at the same time. We both smiled at the same time. We were rich.

It was getting late in the afternoon and the sun was falling down behind the far green hill which with the rock mountain, valleyed the golf course. So we made our way back over the rock mountain, along the railroad tracks, across the field behind our house, through the loose boards in the fence, and went directly into the clubhouse and closed and latched the door behind us.

In the clubhouse, we had found a secret hiding place underneath one of the floor boards. The Marshal kids who had lived there before us had sawed a piece of wood out of the floor and made a cubbyhole. When the board was in place you couldn't tell the hiding place was there. We found it when Bobby brought Samson, the big desert tortoise that they'd also left behind, into the clubhouse and we watched him walk around the floor. The secret board was jimmied up a little and Samson tripped on it. When we pried the board up and found the hiding place, we made a pinkie promise right exactly then: *we would never, under any circumstances including torture, ever divulge the location or future contents of the secret hiding place to anyone.*

We put the five dollar bill in a coffee can and put the can in the secret hiding place. We had no idea what we were going to do with five whole dollars. It was scary to have that much money. But we figured that when we decided what to do with it, with that much money, we could buy about anything we wanted.

We didn't know it at the time, but it wouldn't be too long before we knew exactly what to do with the five dollars.

That night, as Bobby and me lay in bed across the room from each other (the bunk beds were gone and we each had our own bed now), we both dreamed about the same things.

Expeditions. The train tracks. The dairy farm and the black and white cows. The pipes at The 500. The five dollars. The secret hiding place.

Mike and Bobby. On expedition. 1970.

Just before we fell asleep something happened. It was the bad and frightening thing that we had hoped, after moving into a new house, would never happen again.

The first demoralizing realization that raced through our heads when it happened was that we'd been gravely mistaken when we'd thought that a house - like the ones in the small town in Oklahoma - magically made everybody happy and nice. We had believed that houses had some sort of metamorphic ability to wash over people like a tide of kindness and transform them into ideal-people who lived life like the Brady Bunch.

The King was screaming and yelling at Mom again.

Bobby put his pillow over his ears and managed to fall asleep. I lay on my side and stared across the room, out the window, into the backyard at the clubhouse. There was a full moon out that night and the soft light of it flooded over the clubhouse until the shadows began to dance. Very slowly, the clubhouse changed in front of my eyes.

The redwood boards became muscles, the windows became eyes, the varnish became fur and the roof became horns.

Finally, Geronimo Bill's biggest Buffalo was standing in our backyard.

He dipped his head and ate some grass.

Outside our door, down the hall, across the house, Mom screamed.

The Buffalo lifted his heavy head and looked back at me through the bedroom window. There were tears in his eyes.

Bobby dreamt bad dreams that night.

I never slept at all.

The Buffalo came into our room and I had a long talk with him while Bobby slept. He was warning me. He couldn't tell me exactly what was going to happen, but he was sure that I was the only one who would ever be able to figure out what to do about it. I asked him if whatever was going to happen was going to be bad. He nodded his big head, yes. I asked if it was going to happen to me. He shook his head, no.

And then he looked over at Bobby...

STRANGE HUMAN LIKE SHADOWS DANCE ON THE CLUBHOUSE.

SIDE SLATES BULGE TO FORM HEAD

③ WINDOW GETS SMALL — FORMS HIS RIGHT EYE
④ DOOR SHIFTS RIGHT — BENDS TO FORM ROAR
   LEGS + HAUNCHES.

BUFFALO MOVES - SOLIDIFIES TO REAL (MOCK-UP)
END ANIMATION

Another week passed, and then something important happened. It was on an expedition we took along the train tracks in the opposite direction from the way we'd followed them to the golf course. North, as we went, the tracks eventually passed the outside of a small airport named after a man named Whitman. Since nobody ever said anything to us, or tried to kick us out, we used to stand at the fence and watch the planes take off all weekend.

None of the pilots lived in the area, they were all wealthier and from the west end of the valley. Didn't matter though, we shot them all down a hundred times each. They had no idea Bobby and me were master christmas wrapping-paper-tube gunsmiths.

On all of our expeditions, together with our Genuine American Indian Spears, we carried rubber band ammo and our lunch in soapbox-backpacks that we tied shoelace shoulder-straps on. They usually lasted about two expeditions before the string cut through the cardboard and your stuff fell out. But that was okay because by that time Mom was usually done with another box of detergent and the guy whose box broke first got the new one.

Even though all of the places we'd explored up until then still needed more exploring, the discovery we made near the airport was so great, that even if you'd mashed all of the other places together into one monstrous exploring area, it still couldn't compare to the place.

It was behind a public baseball diamond on the east side of the airport. There were hills there; hills that went all the way into some land where there was a sign that said, National Forest. The biggest was about five hundred feet high and had an abandoned telephone pole at the top with a little metal tag on it that said, "GTE pole 7, 12/17/1903" so by the date, we knew they had put it in the ground about the same time when Dinosaurs were around.

Except for the Buffalos and some squirrels and regular birds and stuff, Bobby and me had never seen any wild animals. The big hill instantly became our best and favorite place to explore because there was a family of Red Tail Hawks that sat on the pole watching for mice and squirrels below. They liked to perch up there because from the top of the hill you could see across the entire San Fernando Valley to the Chatsworth mountains at the edge of the world, including our house right behind the police station about six blocks away.

The dirt on the hill was loose but smooth all the way to the bottom where it met the edge of the baseball diamond's left field. Right there, about three hundred feet from the airport runway, there was an old deserted entrance to a mine shaft that formed a makeshift ramp into the air.

There was a certain neighborhood legend, which when we got to the top of the hill and looked down at the tiny dot that was the mine shaft ramp, made our skin feel like two fresh-plucked chickens. The legend said that a kid named Fisher, who had lived in Pacoima years before, took his bike to the top of the hill and rode it down.

Mike and Bobby. Easy Riders. Escaping for the day. 1968.

And hit the ramp. They said he flew three hundred feet.

They said he never landed.

They said he dropped from the air.

Right in front of an airplane.

We didn't know if it was true but we believed it. All the other kids in the neighborhood believed it too, and since Fisher had done the greatest thing anybody had ever heard of, they called him "The King of Pacoima."

Me and Bobby thought about Fisher a lot. We decided

that what he did wasn't so great. He got killed didn't he?

We figured he'd made a good try, but that at some critical moment he had lost all the belief that had gotten him to the top of the hill and then airborne in the first place.

He might have believed he could succeed when he took the first pedal stroke from the top, maybe even halfway down, and maybe even as he hit the ramp. But there had to have been a moment, probably in midair, as he crested the apex of his jump when Fisher lost all faith that he could actually fly.

Bobby, 2nd grade class picture.
Montgolfier Elementary School. 1970.

3

THE WISHING SPOT

"Starlight, starbright, first star I see tonight,
I wish I may, I wish I might, have the wish I wish tonight."
- Traditional

We called the top of the hill The Wishing Spot because we reasoned God would have to hear a wish made that close to heaven. We made a lot of wishes up there, most of which were the kind that never came true; like for a million dollars, or for a time machine, or to be older than we were then. Even though those didn't come true, there were others that did - mostly wishes like for The King to stop yelling at Mom. Although it always started again after a while, at the times we made those wishes the yelling stopped. So we knew beyond any doubt that The Wishing Spot worked, it was just a little too far away from Heaven for God to hear them all.

Bobby and me saw a movie that summer from Walt Disney about two kids who wish to become real live Bear cubs. Through most of the movie we thought it was pretty stupid, until the two kids believed hard enough and then actually turn into what they always wanted to be; two Bear cubs. After that movie, Bobby and me realized that we couldn't wish for anything we really didn't need at The Wishing Spot; wishes like for a million dollars weren't really big wishes at all because we knew, deep down inside, we neither wanted nor needed stuff like that. Whatever we wished for up there we had to need, had to believe in, or else it was really just a lie.

We probably lied more than other kids, but we were different than other kids and had good reasons to lie. We got ourselves in trouble a lot by doing things we knew we shouldn't; like putting a little too much milk on our cereal; closing a front door a little too hard; coughing when we had coughs and knew we shouldn't, which were all things that had evidence connected to them, so we couldn't get out of the punishments for them. And we certainly couldn't lie about them. Since the penalties for these bad things were heavy, the punishment for anything more serious was unbearable. So on those counts, when there was no evidence and it was The King's word against ours, we lied in any way we could to avoid being sentenced to a session with ol' trusty.

We only ever lied to save our hides. And we only lied to The King. Nobody else needed to be lied too. Although, after a while, Bobby and me fancied ourselves pretty good at bending the truth, it was never something we wanted to do. We knew lying was wrong. We knew it was a sin. But other kids never got in trouble for their dreams; they never dreamt a bad thing about The King and worried for days and days whether or not He would know what they'd dreamed.

He did know.

He always knew.

So to us telling the truth and lying meant the same thing because it brought the same results. Except that lying sometimes avoided the hurt; the odds were better. And getting tears in our eyes at an interrogation helped. They came on easy. In those cases lying wasn't everything, it was the only thing.

I lied better than Bobby and sometimes he took the hurt for both of us. We never lied if it meant that someone else would get in trouble, only to save our skins. Most of all we never lied to God.

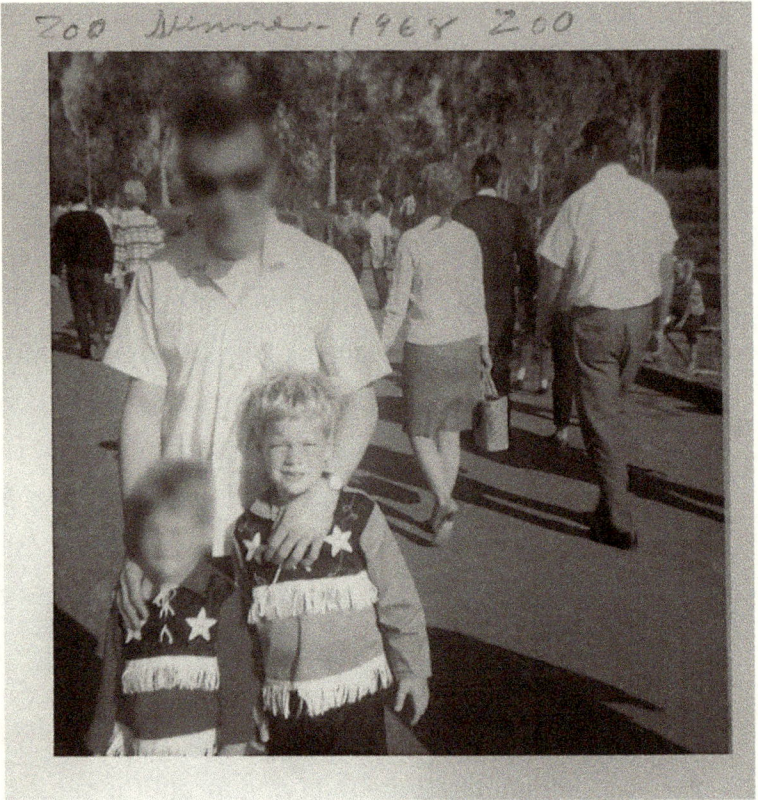

Bobby, Mike and The King. A grand day out. 1968.

As it turned out God would hear a certain wish that we made more than any other wish, and never even knew we did. A wish bigger than the whole country we had come across to discover The Wishing Spot itself.

Even though we never said anything to each other, every time we stood at The Wishing Spot and leaned over the edge of the hill and looked down the giant slope to the mine shaft ramp, and had an imagining in living color that we saw Fisher screaming down the hill, launching into the air and falling from the sky into the propeller of a plane owned by some rich guy from the west valley which scattered Fisher and his bike from the baseball diamond to the runway, we were both always thinking about how to do it right.

Although we were clueless about it at the time, our brains were connected at those moments and we were actually making a collective wish when we were imagining all that. A wish, as it turned out, that would be the most important wish any kid had ever made in the history of the world.

Most of that first summer was okay. We had saved up 20 cents and 40 bazooka bubble gum wrappers, clipped an ad from the back of a comic book and mailed away back east for two bamboo fishing poles. When we weren't catching blue-belly Alligator Lizards with loops in the end of our fishing poles we were swimming in a little corrugated aluminum pool that Mom had saved up her waitress tips to get us.

It was great because at eight and ten it still takes two strokes to actually swim across a pool that size. But the best thing about moving into a house with a backyard was that we got to have a dog. A German Shepherd Dog named Shane. We didn't know what dog papers were, but we knew if your dog had them he was better, so we told everybody that Shane had them. We were sure he did, we just didn't know where he kept them.

Shane went everywhere with us, at least everywhere we could take him. And since most of the places went were exploring places, he went most places.

Shane was really weird for a dog because he thought like a human. He stopped at red lights. Always walked on the sidewalk with us. Never wandered off by himself when we were out at an exploring place, or went to the corner store for a roll of Lifesavers or wax lips. He just sat down and waited for us until we came out. He protected us from punks, and once from some general bigger kids who tried to steal our Genuine American Indian Spears.

Shane. Wise beyond his years. 1969.

We were having a frog-collecting expedition to The 500, with a special frog hunting bucket and rubber gloves. We crawled under the fence beneath the sign that said: *No Trespassing*. The fence was too tall to climb - probably seven feet - and had barbed wire at the top. We crawled under at the spot we always did, where there was a half-hole dug for just such purpose, and Shane was still outside the fence when we got on the other side. Bobby and I held the bottom of it up for him to crawl under.

"Shane, come on, go under." I told him.

He stood there looking at us and blinked with his head to one side like smart dogs do. And then he turned around and walked away.

"Shane! What're you doin'?!" Bobby hollered, because he was scared Shane was running away. But then Shane stopped about 30 feet back from the fence. He turned around and the last thing we saw was this big dirt cloud where his feet used to be.

His paws dug into the ground.

His Batman ears went flat against his head.

His big chest made a giant breathing sound.

Shane jumped.

Shane landed.

It was a big fence, but Shane was a bigger dog.

Bobby and I stood there with our mouths open like we were trying to catch flies or something.

"Damn." It was one of the rare moments when Bobby

and me said a bad word. We couldn't help it. Shane was more like a horse than dog, and smarter than most of the people we knew, kids or grownups.

I reached over and tapped Bobby under the chin with the end of my spear. His mouth closed and we headed into The 500.

Radio Flyer road test. 1970.

When we got to the place where all the drainage pipes emptied out from inside the hills they were buried in, we all stopped.

"Shane, find the frogs." I told him. Shane went up and sniffed a couple of the pipes and when he found the right one he turned around and barked to us. We followed him inside.

We had never been in that particular pipe before and for some reason it was darker and colder than the other pipes. The deeper we ventured, the darker it got. When we looked back, the sunlight cut a slice across the round cement walls and the opening had become about the size of a quarter. So we got out our flashlights and shined them ahead.

And then the squeaks began. More squeaks than we had ever heard in any of the other pipes. A few more steps and the squeaks became more like grunts. It served us right, we had asked Shane to find frogs and he did. Only since Shane never did anything half-way, he had found us the best frogs.

The big frogs.

The two pounders.

The buffalo-frogs.

The really scary ones. These frogs didn't hop away when you came up on 'em, they just sat there looking up at you with their fat eyes, croaking with their big throats bulging out like water balloons.

These were tough frogs.

"Okay, get about ten of 'em." I said as I stuffed the bucket handle into Bobby's hand.

He glanced over at me and said, "Are you crazy? They're man-eaters!" confirming my suspicions about what he was thinking.

"Yeah, they're pretty big. They look like Buffalo turds." I

said. Bobby nodded fast, agreeing a hundred percent a hundred times. The tiny water bison were spread out back into the darkness, and when we shined our flashlights into the pitch black as far as the beams would go, we still couldn't see the end of the herd of them.

"Alright, forget it, she don't want big ones anyway, lets go check out the other pipes." Bobby was already on his way out before I finished.

"She" was The Frog Lady. She lived close to The 500 in a small house set off by itself from any other houses. Although her house was small, her backyard was gigantic. There was a vast, stinky pond in her backyard where she claimed she put the frogs that we sold her for one dollar a bucket.

She said she liked frogs.

We knew she did, we also suspected what she really did with them. And once, not too long after this expedition, we unfortunately found out.

I turned to follow Bobby and Shane out of the pipe and we all three stopped after about two steps. There were four figures coming into the pipe silhouetted against the opening, which was now about the size of a pizza.

We knew we were in trouble instantly, the way kids always know they're in for it when they see bigger kids walking toward them. It's a sixth sense that you lose in later life, but at that moment we still had it, and had it strong, and knew we were as good as dead. We didn't know who these guys were, where they came from, what they were doing at The 500 or why they had chosen this pipe to come in to, but as sure as the frogs behind us were man-eaters we knew we were about to get beaten up.

We shut our flashlights off.

It was so dark that I couldn't see Bobby standing right beside me.

We didn't look back to check for an escape route because there wasn't one. We didn't consider trying to run past them, they were four across and took up the whole pipe side-to-side. And even if we did get past them, they'd chase us down out in The 500 for sure. So we just backed away into the pipe slowly in the slimy water, trying to avoid stepping on any of the buffalo-frogs. But Bobby stepped on one and it croaked, it wasn't hurt; you can't hurt a frog that big. It was mad and the croak was so loud it sounded like the huge bull-cow at the dairy farm.

The croak echoed down the pipe.

We could see the four silhouettes squint into the darkness, and they must have seen us because they started walking quicker.

Their feet splashed faster in the muck.

They were running at us.

They didn't yell or shout or promise they were gonna beat us up or anything. They were silent, and that, we knew, was the mark of death. Punks that scream and holler and say they're gonna beat you up are usually as scared as you are. The ones that don't say anything are serious. So we did the only thing we could think of, we held our Genuine American Indian Spears out in front of us in as threatening a manner as we could muster - scared into forgetting that they were tipped with rubber, not steel.

When they got close enough to where we could see the whites of their eyes, they saw us and laughed. They didn't stop running, they just added laughing to it.

That was it.

We were dead.

Dead and buried.

Bobby screamed, "Mike!"

Suddenly, out of nowhere, out of the darkness along the side of the pipe where you couldn't see anything but the shine off the mossy gook that grew there...

...Shane stepped in front of us.

Shane. The Protector. 1971(?)

The four punks stopped so fast that two of them slipped and fell into the smelly brown stuff at our feet. The other two slid a few feet and when they stopped, they backed away really slow so that each step they took made a sucking sound as they raised their sneakers up out of the mud.

"Nice dog. Easy boy. Nice doggy..." The biggest one said, holding his hands out in front of him and pushing at the air as if that was gonna put more distance between him and Shane.

"No, he ain't a nice dog! And if you touch us, he'll kill you!" I was feeling suddenly very brave, so I said it.

"Yeah!" Bobby added.

Shane took a step toward the two punks in the mud. They scrambled to their feet and Shane bit one of them in the butt.

"Oww!" And he fell down again. Shane stayed still and growled like the lion we had seen in the movie Born Free. Every hair on his neck and back was standing straight up in the air, and in the darkness he looked as big as that Lion. Even we were scared of him right then.

The four punks became silhouettes again and finally disappeared into the light at the end of the tunnel. Shane's hackles went down and Bobby and me hugged him and kissed his big face. He licked us back, so we knew he understood we were saying thank you.

When we came out of the pipe I looked at Bobby and he looked at me and we both said at the same time, "Hey, you look taller."

We took Shane with us whenever we went on expedition to The Wishing Spot because he could climb great. We used to hang onto to his collar and he would pull us up to the top without even trying. He really liked it up there because, I think, it was as close to wild land as you could get in Pacoima and I'm sure he felt at home among the trees and rocks and forest stuff. It was as if when he was up there he was thinking about his relative dogs or wolves and although he wasn't sad about being our dog, I think he probably wanted to know what it was like to live in the wild land by himself, in the same way that Bobby and me always thought about what it would be like to live in one of the Main Street houses at Disneyland.

He would sit near the edge of the big hill at The Wishing Spot and stare out over the valley with this look in his big brown eyes, like the look you get in your eyes when you see something so amazing that your brains turns into sweet cherry jello and you have no control over the way you're looking at it, and you can't look away. I usually got that look when I watched the planes taking off at the airport. Bobby's eyes glazed over like that whenever he looked at our Radio Flyer wagon.

There was another look that Shane would get in his eyes. It was the scariest look on a dog we'd ever seen. Even scarier than when he inflated up like a Lion and made the punks in The 500 drainage pipe run away.

It was a look animals get when you trap them in a corner.

When they are threatened into fighting for their lives.

A survival look.

A wild look.

A look that turned his eyes to big glass aggies.

He only got it when he looked at The King.

Mike, Bobby, our Little Sister, a T-Rex and A Monster. 1971.

4

THE KING OF TERRORS

"...woe to the drunken."
- Isaiah 5:11

When we were kids there were still plenty of things to be afraid of. In those days there were no computers, no video games, no internet.

Monsters still existed.

They hadn't yet been rounded up and banished to the digital realm where you have complete control over them, they still inhabited the same places they had for thousands of years - under our beds. And they abounded in the small and dark places that somehow are always built into houses for the express purpose of hiding them. Killers like the Green-Slime-Puker, the Snake-Headed-Kid-Eating-Hatchet-Woman, the Five-Armed-Worm-Man, and other mutations which - as kids know, yet grownups blame on leaky pipes and stuff - make every single weird sound in the pitch black of the night.

Bobby and me believed in all of the regular monsters that kids are afraid of because, obviously, they existed. These terrifiers included Frankenstein, Dracula, Werewolf, The Bogeyman, The Mummy, The Creature from the Black Lagoon, Godzilla, The Fifty Foot Woman and King Kong. Largely, these guys were needless-to-be-feared because they didn't walk the earth much anymore when we were kids, mostly, by then, they just made movies. However, there were some other, more esoteric mutants that did; like Zombies, Gargoyles, Trolls, Ghouls, Ghosts, Gorgons, Harpys and Hydras. Other kids mostly didn't know about these special monsters, but they were usually the ones that fell prey to them and were never heard from again because they didn't believe. Bobby and me did, and we had secret ways of keeping them away, or if we got caught by one, special ways of banishing them back to the pits of putrid hell-blood from whence they came.

The best way to ensure you didn't fall into the clutches

of these types of demon ilk was to simply avoid the places they dwelled and not summon them into the world.

Inside a closet by yourself? A big fat no.

Under the house? Ut uh.

In our room with all the lights off and the shades drawn? No way.

Watching horror movies alone? Negative.

Repeating a monster's name in a mirror 100 times? Only fools did that.

Playing Ouija board? Instant death.

Camping in the backyard in the pup tent on a full moon? Disaster.

Exploring cemeteries at night? Ha!

Sleeping with your feet dangling off the edge of the bed? May as well cut them off yourself.

Sleeping without the blanket covering every part? Same deal.

Bobby and me had most of the really scary monsters in life handily dealt with; they couldn't get to us because we took precautions, and furthermore they couldn't hurt us if they did because we were the Keepers of the Spell.

We knew all the long-lost ancient rhymes and spells to get rid of individual monsters, but The Spell - the great void-all-monsters defense - was a secret that only we knew. It involved mixing up a special potion of really awful slurpery stuff from a recipe we got for 5 cents out of the back of a comic book. The ingredients were:

A frog. We used a pill bug.

Newt's eyes. All witches recipes have this ingredient. We used marbles.

Bats wings. Same deal. We used a rubber glove.

Locust guano. We looked up guano in the dictionary. We used Samson poop.

Devils weed. We used crab grass.

Pixie wing dust. We cut out the picture of Tinkerbell from my Disneyland map and used that.

Bull sweetbreads. We didn't know what they were, we skipped that part.

Magma. We used dirt.

Goats milk. We used a can of Carnation condensed milk.

Worms. We used worms.

A Potato bug. Bobby and me were Potatobugaphobic. There is nothing more repulsive, useless and disgusting than a Potato bug. We used a Cootie toy.

Brain of Zombie. We used hamburger.

Various household cleaning chemicals.

Mix well over high flame. We did. Once.

It all exploded.

The glop ended up on the kitchen ceiling, the door, the stove, the cupboards, the floor and the sink. And it ended up on us. Covered from head to foot in the anti-monster mixture, Bobby and me took a second to consider the mess. If Mom came home first we were okay, she'd help us clean up what was left after we mopped up what we could before she got there.

We broke out the mop and bucket, and the Spic n' Span. We mopped. We cleaned. We scrubbed. We washed and wiped. We wrung and dabbed and scoured and polished, but the gunk wouldn't come off. Whatever had happened under the lid of the big pot we'd put it all in had turned the stuff into an adhesive the likes of which the Elmers glue company would've paid millions for. It adhered to the walls and it hardened. A piece of it that had florped onto the sink faucet hardened first. I took a spoon and whacked it. It crumbled and fell off. Bingo!

That was the answer, wait until it all hardened and then knock it off and sweep it up. Easy. We saved some of the chunks in a jar - for later reconstitution - to ward off the monsters we were making it for in the first place. The only problem was that it was getting late.

We waited.

And we waited.

The junk was hardening, but not fast enough. The second any spot of it caked up solid, we bashed it off whatever it was stuck to and swept it into a paper bag. We filled one paper bag and got out another. Bobby took the full bag to the garbage while I kept waiting and smacking. When he got back, most of it was gone. There were just two chunky piles of it left on the ceiling. We couldn't reach them, so I boosted Bobby up on my shoulders and he stretched out and took a couple swings at the stuff.

"Higher!" He begged.

"I can't, I'm already on my tiptoes!" I shot back, and then got an idea. I scooted over to the footstool and kicked it under where the stiff lava-soup was plastered to the ceiling. I took one step up the stool and Bobby swung. Crack. He hit it and the stuff dropped to the floor. He jumped off my shoulders and we both sat back against the kitchen wall thinking that we had just avoided the worst session with ol' trusty we ever could've imagined when...

... a car rolled up the driveway.

It wasn't mom's VW bug.

It was the Van.

The King had arrived home first.

The anti-monster potion would never work against The King.

Mom. Doing her best. 1972.

The only thing liable to happen was that he would make us eat it.

In our hearts there was little doubt that what we had been doing was an important and worthwhile effort to save ourselves from the horrors of a possible monster attack, even if deep in our young souls we suspected but could not believe, that these monster were, like for all kids, merely imaginings.

In our minds, the moment we heard the van pull up we

knew that the real threat to our lives every moment, waking or not, was a Monster that was worse than any Thing the combined imaginations of a hundred kids could've produced if asked to build the ultimate mega-monster. We would rather have had to face a killer like that any day, than have to face The King when we had done something we knew he would be angry about.

There wasn't much we could do at that moment except sit there and resign ourselves to our gruesome fate at the end of ol' trusty. Even though we had cleaned up most of the specter-sauce, the kitchen still needed tidying up to ensure He wouldn't notice. There was no time for that. The evidence was clear. The pot was still spackled with the glorp. The stove was flecked with it. The floor had little chunks of it spread all over.

We were doomed.

The only consoling thought that raced through our minds at that moment was the fact that there were no empty beer can portents to what was about to take place. At least it wasn't going to be the kind of thrashing that lasted and lasted and sometimes didn't stop until we passed out. We thanked God for that as we waited for The King to march in.

We heard the garage door open. It closed. And then the music started. Jazz. The King wasn't coming in the house. Maybe he didn't know we were home. Whatever the reason, we knew what he was doing the moment the Jazz faded up.

Now, if there had been any of the crushed empty blue and white cans strewn around the house like tiny dead soldiers before we had started the anti-monster potion, there wouldn't have been enough gold in Fort Knox to pay to stop the whipping we would have suffered. We had learned that empty cans meant full nights of horror. Loud Jazz meant quiet crying. And of course trying to choke back the sobs only inspired the conductor to loftier heights with the baton named ol' trusty. But luckily, even divinely, there had been no such foreshadowing on this occasion.

As quietly as mice in church we wiped the whole room until it sparkled anew. The pot, we washed with a quart of elbow grease. The floor, we swept spotless. We gingerly buried the last bag of monster-repellant deep in a garbage can and covered it with another full bag; the one we used when we cleaned up the backyard after Shane. If nothing else, the evidence would remain undetected and hopefully – prayerfully - the whole mess would just drift away unknown into the past after a few days.

But we couldn't be sure. We checked the kitchen again. It was as it was before the critical mass in the pot had gone supernova.

But we still couldn't be sure. If only the aura of the whole incident lingered in the room after we'd gone, even that, The King would detect. To our perpetual fret, His powers of observation - the ability to look over an empty room and ascertain exactly what had gone on in there up to as much as a week before, especially things that Bobby and me had done - were amplified by orders of magnitude after a bout with the famous libation of beechwood aging.

There was only one thing to do.

Only one chance to thwart His imminent detection of the explosion by way of mental osmosis.

The Wishing Spot.

Bobby and I had to talk to God.

We took Shane with us and slipped noiselessly through the loose boards in the fence.

From The Wishing Spot at the top of the hill you could see the small police station right beside our house. We shared a common wall with the station and, as it turned out, it was as if Mom, Bobby and me were fated to move into that house. If the police station had not been right next door the three of us would've ended up crumpled and cast aside like all the beer cans we bagged up and put in the garage after a night of telltale Jazz. Since the police were so close they were able to get to the house faster than if they'd been called on the phone. They could literally hear everything from the station house; like all of mom's important things being thrown through the living room window into the front yard. They were no dummies those guys. They usually walked over just in time. Usually.

Even so, Mom always took the worst of it, but at the time Bobby and me didn't know the difference between a regular argument and the kind of stuff that went on late at night when we were supposed to be asleep and not hear it. So to us it was all the same. It would have been different if He had been one way when He drank, and another when He didn't; we could've blamed-it-on-the-booze. But it wasn't that way. Under the influence, He was a rage. Sober, He was a perfectionist of such compulsion that nothing pleased him. When you're eight and ten and nothing you do pleases who you're supposed to be looking up to, then everything you do becomes an exercise in complete and desperate futility. And, so it was.

No matter what, Mom protected us from everything she could, but there were times when she couldn't. When it got out of hand, Bobby usually took the scatter-fire. He was younger than me and an easier target, so I guess it was a given that he suffered the slings and arrows while I either had to watch or go outside. Bobby was caught between me, and our baby sister - our half-sister.

At eight and ten years-old his drinking should've been a mystery so complex that Sherlock Holmes at his most cunning would have been baffled into insanity. But it wasn't. We knew exactly why He did it, and it was so simple that we never gave it so much as a second thought after it had first occurred to us.

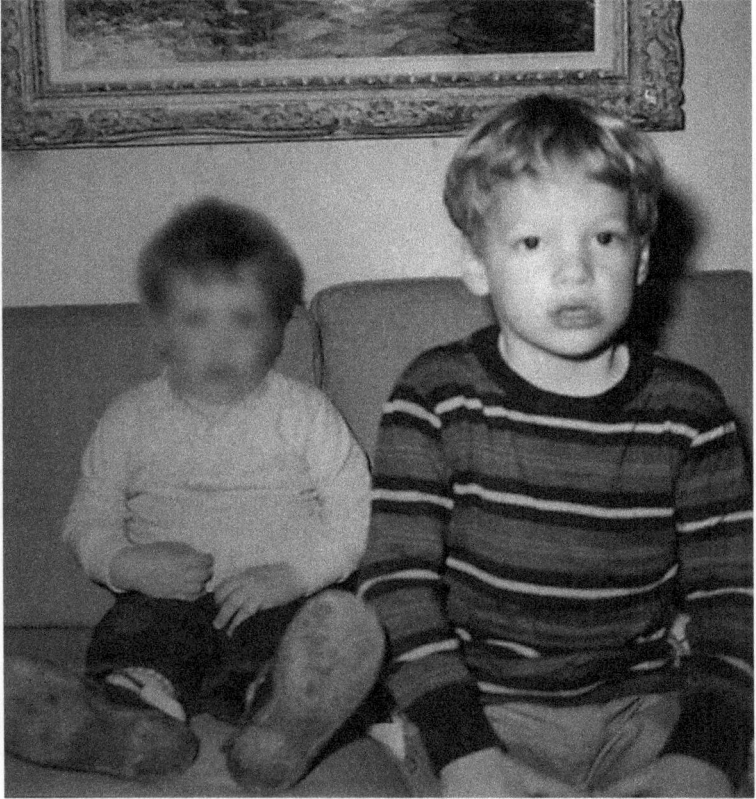

Bobby and Mike. In trouble again without knowing why.
1968(9)?

He drank because the blue and white cans meant more to Him than we did.

But our Genuine American Indian spears meant more to

us than He did, so we were as guilty. Only thing was, that the Genuine American Indian spears were total duds compared to the power of the cans. So because we knew why, we didn't feel any different than other kids.

We didn't pity ourselves the wretched hand we'd been dealt .

We sought no solace from Mom about it. She had it worse than we did .

We did not grow up with inferiority complexes. Or low self esteem.

We did not fall prey to the mental demons of worthlessness He sowed in the furrows of our youthful grey matter.

We wished Him no ill will.

We never devised plans to do away with Him.

We did not hate Him.

We did not love Him.

We neither liked nor loathed Him.

We feared Him.

And feared Him only.

It took no genius to understand that He was unlike the funny, happy-go-lucky drunks in the movies. He was one of the mean kind.

There was nothing He did not know.

There was nothing He could not know.

He was The King of Terrors, and that was that.

Up at The Wishing Spot that night, we wished that he

never find out about the mess we'd made and cleaned up. He never did.

I got it once in a while, but by all rights Bobby never should've survived the war.

I had asked the King a question once, which was really more of a suggestion. An idea which I thought was a really good one. I talked it over with Bobby and he concurred. It was, we thought, a mutually beneficial arrangement which would benefit both me and Bobby and The King.

He didn't think so.

And so Bobby got three broken ribs before I got The Big Idea.

Mom and Bobby. First trip to the Emergency Room. 1968.

5

STICKING UP FOR BOBBY

"My brother didn't hit me, and I didn't hit my brother…"
- Ray Bradbury, The Inspired Chicken Motel.

By design, a younger brother is a tag along. You can pedal faster than he can, walk farther, do all sorts of stuff better than he can by virtue of the fact that you were born two years earlier. You're a little bigger, a little stronger, so you're always waiting up for him at the end of the next block, always looking back to see if he's still there, and always embarrassed of him in front of all your bigger friends.

You shouldn't be, he's your brother, you should look

after him no matter what, be glad to have him with you, and like Mom always said, "Thank God in heaven you have him." But there's a big difference between your friends and your brother. Your brother is always there, you live in the same house, eat at the same table, sleep in the same room, do the same chores, everywhere you are, he is.

Friends on the other hand, are for the daytime. They're different kids, other kids with whom, when you get out of the house, you want to go play. So does your brother, but why should he come when you've already done all that stuff at home with him? He thinks the same thing but (and at ten years-old you have no knowledge of this) in an entirely different manner. He looks up to you. He wants to do the things you do and have the same friends you do because in his eyes you can do no wrong.

If I had told Bobby to jump off a bridge with an umbrella for a parachute, he would've. I never did that, but I did tell him to do something once that I should never have told him to do. "Bobby hop that fence and go get the ball that went over."

"But Hercules is back there." He said.

"Don't worry, he won't get you, he's chained up." The dog was chained up but the chain was thinner than the one we had attached to Samson to keep him from burrowing under our fence back to the Galapagos.

Trusting me completely, Bobby said, "Okay." And over he went. He got the baseball and Hercules got him. Really bad. Twenty stitches bad. Right on the leg.

I learned a valuable lesson that day.

When the thunder of The King's anger befell us (not because of Bobby's injury, but because of emergency room charges) Bobby, who could easily have done so in the midst of his pain, didn't tell on me. He never said I was the one that had told him to jump the fence.

Even though he didn't know what it was, at eight years-old Bobby had honor; a character trait that I, at times, sadly lacked on his behalf. If the tables had been turned and I had been mauled I still don't know if I would not have snitched on him.

As years pass and you learn the irreplaceable value of a brother, you make valiant attempts to retrieve all of the brotherly history that has since run under the bridge of regret. Luckily because of the Hercules incident I realized early on that I only had one brother, and one brother alone.

Bobby and I were closer than other brothers because of the common enemy we shared. At home it was literally a matter of life and death, so I watched his back and he watched mine. Survival bred dependency and that, in turn, bred closeness.

But as that first summer wore on towards school time in September I sometimes dropped the ball. When I did it wasn't out of a lack of love for Bobby, it was out of fear of winning something that no kid must ever win. Something almost as bad as having your own Dad hate you: peer disapproval.

Peer approval, its close relative, is important but it's easy to win. You swallow a bug and you're a hero. Disapproval is so horrifying that you do anything to avoid it, even crush your little brother's feelings.

"C'mon Mike, geez hurry up." They would say.

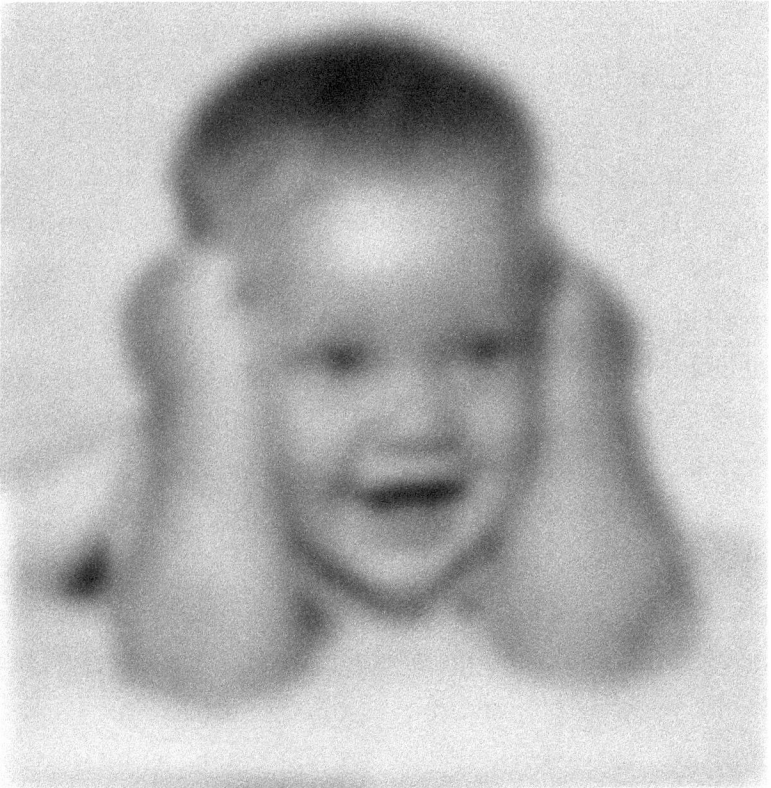

Bobby. Born happy. 1964.

"I am, just hold it, my brother's comin'." I would answer.

"Why'd you have to bring him anyway?" They would ask.

I never answered. It was a terrible sin: brotherly silence. Bobby would've stuck up for me, that was his nature. Mom always said Bobby had been born with the happy gene, a naturally sunny outlook that even under the dark clouds of abuse never dimmed.

Years before we moved there, Pacoima had become integrated. Bobby and me didn't know what white-flight was or what it meant, but we knew it had started in the area because we heard Him say something about it to Mom once. He hated having to live in a house that someone moved out of because of white-flight. We thought it was a disease or something, which it turned out to be; it made neighborhoods sick and houses cheaper. To grownups, the world was black and white and a few other colors, to us it was all green.

That summer there were nine kids on our block. Chad and Ferdie lived across the street from us. Chad was a boy's size 14 husky and Ferdie was a bookworm. Their Dad was a salesman and gone most of the week, every week. Their mom, we were convinced, was glued to the recliner chair in front of their television. She ate chocolates. Through their screen door we could see her; a monstrous shaded whale, beached in a big Barcalounger. In between chocolate-mouthfuls she would grab a CB radio microphone and shout into it, trying to find her husband.

"Martin?! Marty I know you can hear me, Marty! If you're over at the Blue Hotel bar again, don't you dare come home, 'cause I can tell what you've done by the stupid grin on your face!"

The other kids were spaced out down the block. There were two Raymonds; little Raymond was a nice kid, big Raymond was a gang member and he wore heavy wool shirts buttoned to the neck in the middle of summer, which we just couldn't understand for the life of us. The Hernandez brothers, Hector, Raul and Rudy lived at the end of the street. Hector was a lot older and a lot bigger than any other kid on the block. So naturally he used to beat the tar out of us. Raul hung around with big Raymond and Rudy had a transistor radio surgically affixed to his ear so he never missed a Los Angeles Dodger's game.

None of them liked me or Bobby. First, they blamed us for kicking out the Marshal kids who had lived in the house before us. Anyone who dumps on your buddies is your enemy, right? And second, the reason they honestly, truly hated us is that we were easy to pick on.

Mike, Mom and Bobby. Music lessons. And a smile. 1969.

It was no secret what went on at our house, loud Jazz, loud screaming, loud crashes when furniture went through the windows, normal stuff. So our lot in life, even before the prerequisite of death, was already in the public domain.

There were even times when the Grand Inquisitor held court in the front yard, so everyone knew and therefore in the eyes of the Telfair Ave. death squad, we were a couple of pathetic mongrels whom they could kick around and who would never dare bite back for hopes of a morsel of friendship someday. Who's easier to kick around than somebody who has already been softened up for you? We were easy prey and there were too many of them to fight back against.

We did all sorts of things to escape the horrors of the neighborhood; expeditions with Shane, frog collecting, golf ball barter, and when school finally started, we discovered something new.

We noticed that everybody dropped their pop bottles along the boulevard on the way home. In those days, when aluminum cans were a thing of the future and recycling meant nothing to nobody, you bought your soda in a bottle and tossed it when you were through. Bobby and me, however, fathomed the cash flow opportunity in the gutters. It didn't matter what kind or size of bottle, they all had a deposit on them. Osborne Blvd. was the most frequented route home from school for all the kids from the surrounding neighborhoods and it was an untapped gold mine.

Using the Radio Flyer we collected soda bottles from Pacoima Jr. High to the police station (about 20 blocks) and from the Jessup dairy farm to our school, Montgolfier Elementary (about 30 blocks). Sometimes there were so many that we had to make two trips from the boulevards to the White Front Supermarket or the Dales Jr. Mart to cash them in.

After a number of collection runs like this, I devised a modification for the Radio Flyer. With a few pieces of scrap wood and some metal screws we built stake-bed sides for it. When we finished it, Bobby got that look in his eyes again. Only this time it was an even more far away look. It was now like the distant look in the eyes of the Golden Eagle with the broken wings we saw once in a cage too small for it to fly around in at the L.A. Zoo. There was something sad and wishful about the Eagle's look; a look brimming with hope that someday a careless zookeeper would forget to latch the gate after feeding time, that its wounded wings would magically heal and catch the wind once more, and carry him away back to the place he was most happy.

The stakes were about two feet high and increased the carrying capacity of the wagon about three times. Now we could really haul.

In two weeks Bobby and me had made about seventeen dollars! We had no idea it was that much because when we redeemed bottles we would normally only get about two dollars, which we promptly stuck in the special coffee can and hid back in the secret hiding place underneath the floor boards of the clubhouse. We never kept track of how much money we were taking in when we got it, because there would've been no surprise when we counted it. But when we finally did we flipped out! With the five dollars from the golf ball trade, that made twenty two dollars.

We were millionaires, plain and simple.

For some reason, an important reason that was a fear that someday we would really need the money for something more important than anything else in the world, we never spent the twenty two dollars. It was our stash. Our hedge against a type diabolical inflation the sole indicator of which was the dreaded Jazz music which spilled from the forbidden place - the garage.

With the twenty two dollars safely cubby-holed, we decided that we would spend whatever else we made on the greatest things in life.

Pez dispensers. I got Popeye. Bobby got Bozo.

A six-pack of wax bottle cokes.

Fizzer candy.

A couple Viewmaster wheel slides; they were a must because we had looked at the only two we had (of the Grand Canyon and Disneyland) so many times that we'd burned holes in the little picture parts from holding them up to the light so many times.

A styrofoam Soaring Sam airplane.

Comic books. Bobby got Hawkman, I got Captain America.

A giant cow bone from the Butcher at Dale's Jr. Mart for Shane.

Hot Wheels. Bobby got a Red Baron. I got a Blue Flame.

Great things were more important to us than to other kids. To them they were just toys, used and then discarded after the novelty wore off. To Bobby and me these were articles more precious than all the treasures of The Pirates of the Caribbean because we worked to get them, because they weren't handed to us (although Mom would've gladly spoiled us rotten had she had the money) so we both had a genuine appreciation for what was ours and what was someone else's. We respected not so much what a thing was as what it meant. The great stuff we secretly bought with the extra money from the pop bottles was the stuff that made life worth living. They weren't just diversions, they were the essence of our lives.

With all of the great stuff safely stockpiled we dedicated the rest of the money to going to the movies.

We learned fast that if we wanted to hold on to what would sometimes amount to three whole bucks (movies were 75 cents then and a big pop bottle was worth a dime) we had to hide it in our shoes because the inevitability of getting beaten up on the way home was a surer thing than six empty cans equaling another night when would come the screams and yells.

Saturday was movie day. It was a short bus ride to the Panorama Cinema, but we loved it because we were out by ourselves and far enough away from the neighborhood Huns to feel safe and like little big shots. If we had made a particularly good haul with the bottles that meant Milk Duds or Sugar Daddies and Coke.

We always sat down front because being that close to the screen, it felt like you were inside the movie.

About the best movie we ever saw there was The Seventh Voyage of Sinbad, which had the absolute best thing anyone ever thought up for movies - Diorama! At the time we didn't know that Dinosaurs had been extinct for tens of millions of years and of course believed that monsters in general existed, so animated clay Cyclopses and Centaurs were undoubtedly real and posed as great a threat as did The King of Terrors.

The only difference was the defense against them.

With killer-Diorama-bad-guys we only had to close our eyes and they were powerless, with the King we only had The Wishing Spot, and it was too far away to get to when we needed it most.

Mike and Bobby. Just before the road trip to California. 1967.

Back then theaters never cleared the house after a movie, so if we got there for the matinee we could stay and watch the same movie three or four more times before we had to go home.

We went to see The Seventh Voyage of Sinbad on three consecutive Saturdays. So we had the chance to know every frame of the movie, every monster that threatened Sinbad, and every trick he used to beat them. In the end of the movie, Sinbad and the Princess fly away on a magic carpet. That was very important. And we never forgot that.

On one certain really hot day (the third of the three Saturdays) Bobby and me went to the corner to wait for the bus to the Panorama theater. The bus rolled up on time and we put our change in the change-thing and turned to find a seat just as the bus lurched forward back onto Osborne Blvd. When we looked into the back of the bus, our hearts hit our shoes and our stomachs flew away.

There, in the very last seats, were the four Punks from The 500 drainage pipe.

The one that Shane had bitten on the butt walked up the aisle and dragged us back to his buddies. It was a busy traffic day and the Bus Driver never saw a thing.

We got off the bus at the theater with a matching set of black eyes and no money. They had taken our pop bottle cash and laughed when they hit us.

The ticket man at the theater knew us pretty good by then and when he saw our black eyes he let us in for free.

We watched The Seventh Voyage of Sinbad, for the tenth, eleventh and twelfth times. When we came out of the theater it was almost dark and we didn't have any bus fair. Mom was working late, and calling The King for a ride home was so stupid an idea that it never even entered our heads. So we walked. It was a long, long way and took us about three hours.

As we walked, the sun went down and the moon came out. It was a crystal clear night and the stars were shining like diamonds. Bobby and I thought a lot but did not talk on the way home.

It was then, when I was watching the stars pass above us as I was thinking about life in general and about home and about the four Punks and mostly about Bobby and The King, when it was getting toward the end of the year when Bobby was nine and I was eleven, that I received, as if from above, the greatest, scariest, best idea that any kid in the history of all time ever had.

That's when I got...

The Big Idea.

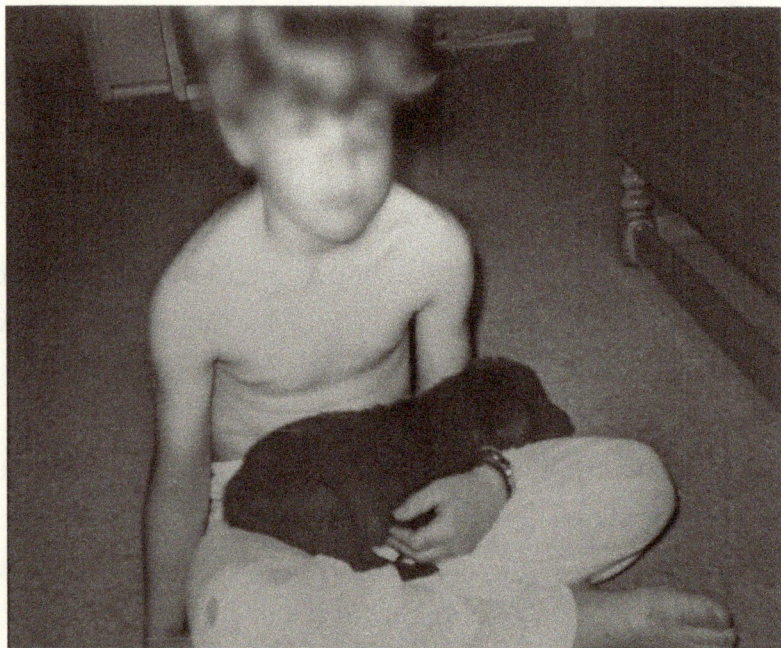

Bobby. A black eye, and a puppy named, "Sorry." 1971.

6

THE BIG IDEA

"When your heart is in your dreams, no request is too extreme."
- Jiminy Cricket

Before anybody ever loses the innocence of youth there are a few magical things, impossible in later life, that can still happen. The reason these things are lost to the grownup world is at once simple and incomprehensible: in the quick second between the age of twelve and your thirteenth birthday, the great secrets to them all are replaced in your mind with thoughts of love.

It is not like the nagging forgetfulness of old age, instantly it is as if the great secrets never existed and are therefore ever-after doomed to be denied.

There are seven of these lost secret fascinations and abilities:

1. Animals can talk.

2. Your favorite blanket is woven from a fabric so mighty, that once pulled over you head-to-toe it becomes a impenetrable force-field with which you can disappear at will.

3. Nothing is too heavy to lift with the aide of a red cape.

4. Your hand held fore finger out and thumb up actually fires bullets.

5. Jumping from any height with an umbrella ensures complete safety.

6. Monsters exist and can be both seen and done battle with. And the greatest, most special and regrettable loss of all...

7. The ability to fly.

Bobby. Flight training. 1972.

The corollary to all this is the eventually lost instinct that all kids have. It is buried deep in the subconscious until it's forced to the surface. It is a reminder, a fail-safe that prevents you from ever mentioning the seven abilities to anyone over the age of thirteen.

Although virtually foolproof, there are times when the overwhelming excitement of having just fired a live round from your finger, or lifted a three ton boulder is too much to take and you unthinkingly blurt out the accomplishment to a grownup only to be laughed at and ridiculed. This is why the instinct is there. Yet it serves a higher purpose still, and that is that witnessing first hand the profound disbelief that grownups have in the seven lost abilities, you have no choice but to know that someday you too will suffer the same fateful amnesia. Therefore, bright kids take hold of the seven great abilities and fascinations and savor the very seconds and minutes and days of them knowing full well their time is, at best, fleeting.

This is the way Bobby and me felt.

This more than anything else is why we relished both the great treasures in life and the seven secret abilities. Of course, since we were nine and eleven none of the seven abilities were lost to us. We had complete and direct command over them all and could invoke them at will to use in any manner we saw fit.

Talking to animals was easiest, we talked to Shane all the time and he talked right back. Utilizing our blankets as vanishing force-fields was next in order, we practiced this ability weekly when the screaming and yelling would start at night.

Lifting incredibly weighty objects was a breeze with my red Flag-O'-America blanket cinched around either of our necks. However, we knew this ability to be particularly unique and did not abuse the privilege.

In the same way, we knew that although our hand-guns certainly worked, our ammo supply was limited and not to be squandered.

On the matter of umbrella-'chuting we knew little. We didn't have an umbrella and a situation desperate enough to warrant a jump with one never presented itself. But still we had faith that if we ever had to employ it, it would work without a hitch.

Monsters we saw nightly and did battle with as frequently. This was a given in life and you did your best against them or perished.

Even as a kid, when belief in the fantastic comes easy, mastery of the impossible is ordinary, and astonishment is common place, the last ability was a skill of such enormity that it commanded a reverence which teetered on the edge of disbelief. Although the facility is indeed reserved for kids - and kids only - not many ever attempt it, let alone accomplish the feat.

It was usually when we were in the clubhouse working on the Radio Flyer that Bobby would get that far away look in his eyes, and would ask me, "Whadda you think? You think you can fly?"

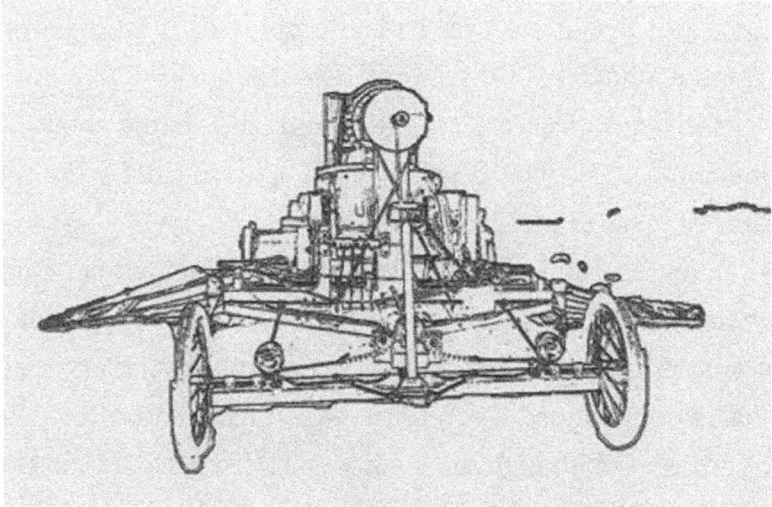

The Flyer. Preliminary design #1.

It was the toughest question a kid could get. If I had said, "No" then I was as bad as the grownups. If I had said "Yes" and been asked to prove it and subsequently could not, Bobby would've lost faith in me. That could not be allowed to happen because we depended on each other too much, so I usually answered, "Yeah I guess probably." It was a safe reply, not too concrete, not too ambiguous, right down the middle.

Bobby's outlook on the matter was somewhat similar to mine, but had one major difference; he could fly alright, he believed, that was not the thing of it. Bobby believed that of all the seven lost abilities, flight was the one which came most naturally. To him it was not the most incredible, it was the easiest.

"You ever done it?" I asked once.

"Of course. Couple times." Bobby said as offhanded as if I'd asked if he knew how to breathe.

"When?" I said like I didn't believe him, but I did.

"Some times." He answered in a way that made me feel like I was his little brother.

Bobby knew something I didn't, I was sure of it. "How?" I asked.

"With the Soaring Sam, of course, but it ain't big enough. Can't go too far."

"Mean you didn't just do it like Superman?"

"No. Superman's only in comic books, he ain't real. Ya can only do it with some kind of Flyer." Bobby lessoned.

"Mean like a plane?"

"No, don't need a plane, just a Flyer."

"What's the difference?"

"Geez, Mike, whatsa matter with you? A plane's a plane. A Flyer's a Flyer. Plane's need all that plane stuff. Flyer's don't need nothing." This was news to me. But to Bobby it was all so obvious that he didn't even look at me when he spoke, he just kept polishing the sides of the Radio Flyer and although it was right in front of his nose, he never noticed.

It all came together for me real slow.

The realization was like a disappearing island, when the ocean was up it did not exist, but when the tide was out, there it was.

A plane was a plane.

A Flyer was something else completely.

The day after we'd been beaten up on the bus and had had our pop bottle money stolen, a Sunday - the hottest day of that whole year, over 100 degrees - and after I'd thought about Flyers harder than I'd ever thought about anything, I told Bobby, "Come out to the clubhouse with me, I wanna show you something."

We went in and closed and latched the door. The King was still asleep; we knew why because on the way out back we passed the garage door and the smell of the cans leaked out and told us why. In the clubhouse it smelled half sweet and half like gasoline. The varnish on the outside was soft from the heat and seeping through the spaces between the boards and running down the inside walls. It looked like the clubhouse was crying. Not hurt crying, but sad crying as if the clubhouse knew what I was gonna ask Bobby.

I pulled the wagon out to the middle of the floor.

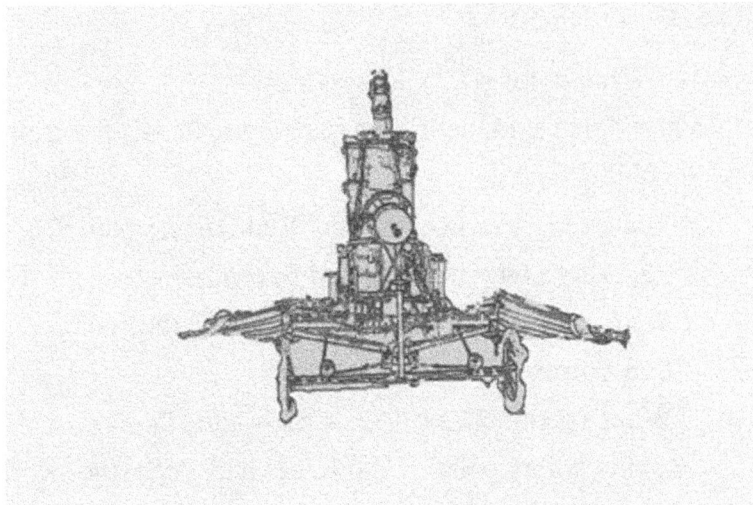

The Flyer. Preliminary design #2.

"Well, what did you wanna show me?" He asked.

"Look at the wagon." I said, and he did.

"Yeah, so?" Bobby stood there staring at it for a minute, but he still didn't get it.

"What color is it?" I asked him.

"Red." He said, as if I was getting light headed from the smell of the varnish.

"Yeah, red. What color is the Red Baron's plane?"

"Red, that's why he's the Red Baron." Bobby sighed.

"Yeah, red. Who's the greatest flyer of all time?"

"Red Baron."

"What's it say on the side of the wagon?"

Bobby knew what it said, he had seen the words a hundred thousand times before, but still - probably because he knew what I was getting at all at once and it was too much for his brain - he got down on his knees and stuck his face close to the side of the wagon and read the words. There was another bruise on Bobby's back that I saw when his shirt slid up as he knelt down.

"R-a-d-i-o F-l-y-e-r." He said it so slow he almost just spelled it.

"Flyer..." I echoed.

It all at once became as clear to me as the view from The Wishing Spot why Bobby always got that journeying look in his eyes whenever he touched or looked at the wagon.

"Yeah... Flyer." He said again and looked up at me, wondering why after he'd done some flying and I hadn't, that I had gotten the idea before him. But he knew. He knew I loved him. And since I was two years older, it was right that I had thought up The Big Idea.

"Thanks, Mike." And that was the last that was ever said about it.

And then someone died. He and his father went away for a long time. Since they were grownups and since the place they went to attend the funeral was so far away, they had to take a plane. A new kind of plane called a 747. Even though it was a gigantic plane that could carry hundreds of people across entire oceans to far away places, the 747 plane was no Flyer.

It could go up in the air.

It could fly.

But eventually, sometime, no matter what... it had to come down.

Those three weeks were very strange. No worry. No screaming and yelling. No hitting. No peeking under the locked garage door. And most incredible of all, no Jazz.

Jazz, depending on the artist, but more so by the selection, had become the clockwork of hurt by the volume of which we could prophecy the amplitude of the night's screaming to come. The music was a barometer whose mercury, like the knot of fear in our guts, rose quickest under the pressure of Take Five, by Dave Brubeck.

During those three weeks Mom worked days, I babysat our little sister and Bobby started collecting the parts for The Big Idea. This is what was on the list I gave him:

1. Plywood and 2 by 4's.

2. A seat from a baby stroller

3. A bicycle sissy bar

4. Two front bike wheels and two back bike wheels

5. The wing from our styrofoam "Soaring Sam" airplane

6. A go-cart steering wheel

7. Two "Cox" airplane engines

8. A lawn mower engine

9. Two bike chains

10. A lot of tape

11. A lot of glue

12. Little kid bike training wheels

13. Two empty coffee cans

14. One mile of string

15. A motorcycle helmet

16. Two paper kites with long rag tails

17. My "Snoopy" lunch box and thermos (In case you get hungry or thirsty)

18. Two pairs of socks, underwear, your warm jacket

19. Three "Highlights" magazines (in case you want to read something)

20. Some postcards and donuts

21. Samson (so you don't get lonely)

22. The Cheerio's box "Pin hole" camera (so you can take pictures)

23. My lucky rabbit's foot

24. Your Davy Crocket coon skin cap

25. My Disneyland map (so you don't get lost)

26. Nails and Screws

27. And most important of all, our <u>RADIO FLYER</u> wagon.

When I got done with the list and looked it over, my heart sank. Some of the things that we didn't have (the Cox airplane engines, the kites and the donuts and postcards) were going to cost money, money that for a forgetful second I was sure we didn't have. Until I remembered the cubbyhole secret hiding place.

The nagging feeling that we'd both carried around with us - that someday we were going to need that twenty two dollars for something more important than anything else - was now clear.

It was money to be spent for the sole purpose of seeing The Big Idea through to the end.

I helped to get some of the stuff, but Bobby went out and got most of it by himself. We hid it all in separate areas of the clubhouse so that if any of it was discovered before we finished The Flyer we would only lose that part and not the others. We also bought a Master lock for the door and tacked cardboard up in the windows so no one could see inside.

About this time, when He had been gone for ten days, Mom got a second waitress job at night. When she was gone and our little sister was asleep we went out to the clubhouse and worked on The Flyer.

Since we didn't have any tools we had to use The King's. Using the King's tools was absolute suicide, but we didn't have a choice; besides, we

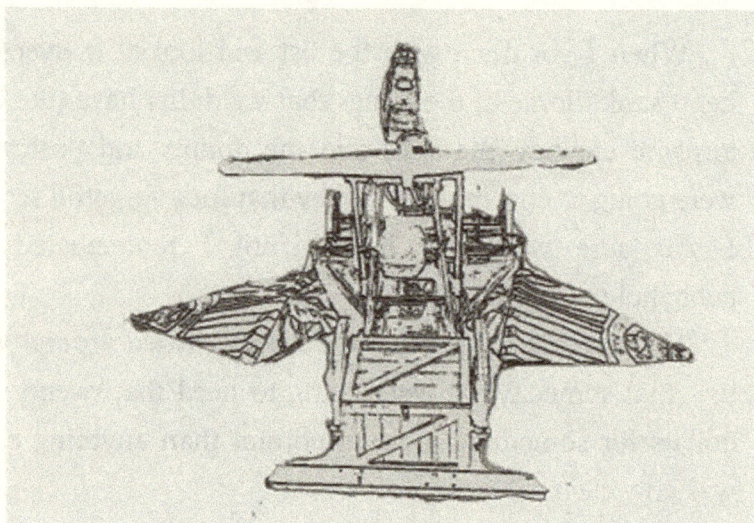

The Flyer. Preliminary design #2. Rear section.

figured to be done and have Bobby on his way a full day before He came home. I would take the thrashing for using the tools but that was no big deal because my thrashing wouldn't be half of the one Bobby would get if he was still here. Even so, when we were done we tried to put the tools back in exactly the same spots we took them from, and hoped He wouldn't notice.

But we knew he would.

Even if He didn't notice He would say He did to check for guilt on our faces - which we would hopefully be able to lie our way through – so just in case, to lessen the brunt of the wrath, we took out some insurance in the form of hiding ol' trusty, - the detachable electric cord to the Corningware percolator coffee pot. We weren't stupid, when it got down to the brass tacks it was always better to strapped with a belt.

It took six days to build The Flyer.

On the seventh day we ran out of wood.

That left four days before the 747 brought Him back.

During those last four days Mom seemed happier. She was tired from the two jobs, but I think she thought that somehow, probably by the grace of Saint Ann (who she always prayed to when she took out her Mother's special ring from its secret hiding place), He would be changed when He came back; that maybe the ordeal of the funeral would have been an experience so sobering that on the plane flight back he would have examined his own life and changed for the better.

Three days before His return The Flyer still needed side safety rails. Since we'd run out of wood, we waited until it was dark and went through the loose boards in the redwood fence and commandeered two of the pallets in the field behind our house.

The 1 by 4's fit perfect. We just nailed them right on.

Even though we took the pallets at night, somebody had seen us. Probably Chicky Erskine, the sour, squash-faced wife of our next door neighbor who spent most of her waking hours spying on and making life miserable for us because we had once had a Freddie Blassie/John Tolos wrestlefest on her side lawn.

Anyway, the word got out about, "Something those new kids are hiding in their shed..." So we had to start standing guard at the clubhouse all day and all night in case someone tried to steal The Flyer or worse, bust it to pieces.

Busting things to pieces is a kid's law, and the collective conscience of the Telfair Ave. death squad held this law near to its heart: breaking things to smithereens is always better than stealing. They didn't know exactly what was in there, but we had it, they didn't, so they would either possess it, or be sure that we couldn't.

They all tried; Chad and Ferdie and the Hernandez kids and Big and Little Raymond. They devised elaborate plans to try and coax us out of the backyard so they could break into the clubhouse; they pretended to be our friends; tried bribing us with baseball cards; and when all these failed, they resorted to force. But every time they got within even ten yards of us Shane appeared.

We didn't know if Shane knew exactly what we were doing, or what we had in the clubhouse, but he knew that it was important - that it was ours and that no one else should have it. He protected us and he protected The Flyer. But because Shane was so diligent about keeping them out they all figured that what was in the clubhouse must've been something infinitely more valuable than they'd first thought. It made them more determined. So much so that Chad and Ferdie crumbled under envy-of-the-unknown and did something that would normally have branded them as rats for the rest of their lives.

They told their mom.

So the worst thing that could ever happen, happened.

Chad and Ferdie's mother called up the police and complained that she had heard from a friend of a friend, that there existed the possibility, which may or may not be true, but was not altogether unlikely, that Bobby and me were hiding stolen televisions in the clubhouse, and, "By God!" she wanted something done about it.

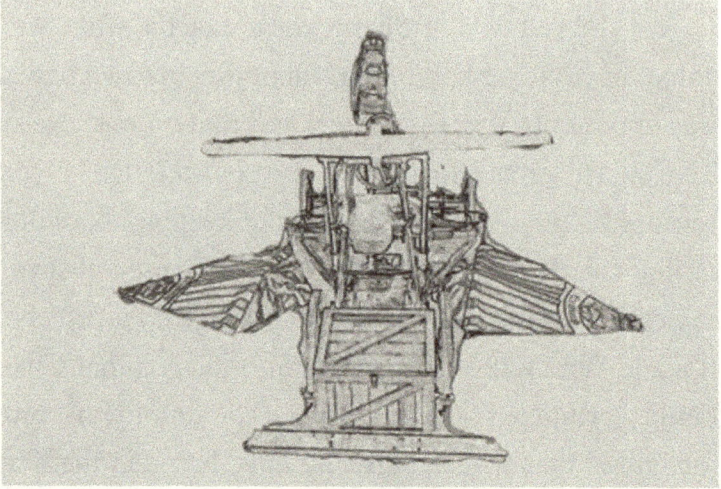

The Flyer. Colored pencil rendering.

It almost spelled the end of The Big Idea.

If the police came, it would be discovered. They would tell The King when he came back. And even though the police would think they were doing their job - which they would have been - they would be unwittingly sentencing us both to death.

Not only had we used The King's tools, we had jimmied the lock on the old construction shack in the field behind our house. Out of it, we had taken the lawn mower engine. Even though the engine had been there for about twenty years and didn't work until I fixed it; even though the guy that owned it was probably dead by then; even though nobody else on the planet earth even knew it was there, they would call it stealing.

There would be nothing we could say - even if we

divulged the entire plan of The Big Idea - that they would believe. But it wasn't the police we were worried about.

In The King's mind, stealing, or even just being accused of stealing was a capital offense, for which only one special and often threatened, but until then never dealt out, punishment would do.

He would kill us both.

The Flyer. Construction complete.

7

THE FLYER

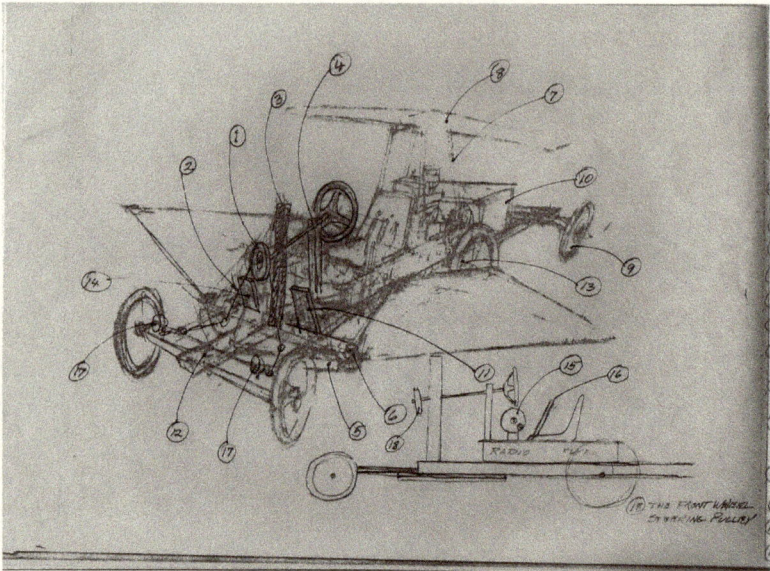

"Gravity, Lift, Thrust and Drag."
- The Forces That Affect Flight.
(Well, the forces that affect the flight of an airplane
anyway)

It didn't take long for the fear about what the police might say if they found The Flyer to turn into total panic. It took about ten seconds. We had to hide The Flyer, and hide it fast. Even though Shane had kept anyone from seeing inside the clubhouse, and nobody knew what was in there, it was no longer safe. It was suspected, and that was more than enough to make us realize that The Flyer had to be moved to top secret quarters.

But where?

The same day we heard that Chad and Ferdie's mom had made up the story and told it to the police was two days before The King was due back. We took Shane and Samson and barricaded all four of us inside the clubhouse for an emergency meeting. The situation was as desperate as war, and war is what we considered it. We had to find a place where nobody ever went, where nobody would look, a place where we could leave The Flyer without having to worry about it getting stolen or busted into scrap.

The first hundred places we thought up were stupid and obvious: the field behind our house, the big-frog pipe at The 500, our room, The Wishing Spot... these were all no good. But when we considered The Wishing Spot something else occurred to us; wherever we were going to hide The Flyer had to be close enough to the big hill with the telephone pole, so when we took it up there to do The Big Idea we wouldn't have to waste time retrieving it and then pulling it all the way to the airport.

That's when the perfect place came into our heads at the exact same time.

The old mine shaft.

It was right at the edge of the baseball diamond's left field, and by the condition of the plywood that was nailed across the front we knew it had been abandoned for at least a million years. All of the wood was still in place and there was no graffiti or vandalism, so we knew nobody ever went in there to explore or anything. Even Bobby and me, who were expedition experts, had never gone in there. Mostly because of the big sign across the top of it that read: "DANGER! CONDEMNED! NO TRESPASSING! 6 MONTHS IN JAIL AND $5,000.00 FINE!"

But now, considering the critical situation we were in, these consequences seemed puny compared to what would happen if the police came and snitched on us to The King. And anyway, if we did get caught in the mine shaft we figured jail was better than death, and the 5,000 dollars was just a couple of good pop bottle hauls. So all things carefully weighed, the decision was made, The Flyer was going to the mine shaft.

There, it would be concealed and safe.

Having to go to school from 8 a.m. to 3 p.m. had thrown a serious monkey wrench into our building schedule, and added to that the information about the police we had found that day, it was a miracle that we finished at all. We'd completed construction that Tuesday night, just 12 hours before we learned about the snitching. So because we'd finished later than we thought, we anticipated there wasn't going to be any time for a test flight. No matter, we thought, The Flyer was solid and Bobby had flown before; and we would be in contact for sometime after initial takeoff via the Yuban coffee can telephone I'd built from instructions in a Boy's Life magazine, so any problems that arose, I could advise Bobby on before he hit the higher altitudes.

Although construction was done, having to stand sentry to thwart an unexpected attack on The Flyer all the week before had slowed down the assembly to a crawl. Only being able to work on The Flyer in short bursts meant that we hadn't done three important things: we hadn't bought the donuts and postcards and we hadn't yet written the note to Mom. So we had to push the launch date back until the day after He came home.

He was due that Friday.

We had planned on that Thursday because then Bobby would only have missed school on Friday, which was no big deal because all we ever did on Fridays at Montgolfier Elementary was watch propaganda movies produced by the Los Angeles Unified School District that tried to convince us that Ketchup was a vegetable.

As we prepared to move The Flyer to the mine shaft entrance late that Wednesday night, we discussed moving the launch date back to the next best day, Saturday. Bobby was nervous about it because that meant launching on a day when The King was home and any number of things could happen, the worst of which was that He would discover the whole Big Idea and somehow stop it.

"It has to be on Saturday, that's better anyway because then you won't be absent at school on Friday." I told him.

"Wouldn't matter, never do nuthin' on Fridays." Bobby countered.

"But we can't get the donuts and postcards till after school on Friday. And we still gotta write Mom the note." I reminded him.

"Yeah, I know... but what happens if -"

"- Don't worry, He ain't gonna find it. He's never even been over to the airport and He sure ain't got no reason to go in the mine." The whole plan sounded better to me as I talked it out.

"Yeah, I guess." Bobby had a different look in his eyes now. It was a sad look and it made me think of the Big One at Geronimo Bill's Buffalo Farm in Oklahoma.

"Okay, look, this is the plan. First we move The Flyer to the mine shaft and nail it inside. Tomorrow and Friday we just act normal. Friday after school we go to the Yum-Yum's and get the donuts. Then we take the bus to the old store near the mission and get the postcards. On Saturday we go to the Panorama movies and see Sinbad a couple more times. Then we come back home and eat dinner. Then we say we're gonna go to bed early and go in our room. We lock the door and write the note for Mom. Then we sneak out the window and go to the mine and get The Flyer and take it up to The Wishing Spot. And then, we do The Big Idea."

As I listed it all in order like that, it sounded foolproof. It must've sounded good to Bobby too, because he looked a little less sad.

"Yeah, okay, I guess that'll work pretty good." He said.

"It will, here..." I held both of my little fingers up in the air, "I double pinkie promise." A pinkie promise was one thing, and it meant eternal shame for the person that broke it, but a double pinkie promise was something altogether different. It was even more serious than a blood oath, and the pledge made Bobby's eyes widen for a second. We slowly locked fingers, and then I swore that I wouldn't let anything go wrong. After a double pinkie promise, I couldn't.

It was extra dark that night, and when I stepped outside to see if the coast was clear I noticed there was no moon in the sky, just stars. There was nobody around, we were safe, we had to move The Flyer right then.

I gave the secret knock on the door:

Tap tap-tap-tap-tap... tap-tap

Bobby came out with Shane and Samson. We connected Samson back up to his long chain and told him not to worry, that we would be back for him. I set the piece of plywood we used as a ramp out the clubhouse door and Bobby wheeled The Flyer out into the backyard. It was the first time it had seen the real world and it was beautiful. All of the modifications were finished and for a moment we stood there staring at it in the light of the back porch bulb.

The stroller seat was bolted to the plywood base and the sissy bar was tied onto the seat so Bobby would be able to relax when he reached cruising altitude. We had switched out the wagon wheels for the bike wheels (big ones in back, small in front) to help takeoff speed on the loose dirt of the big hill, and had the rear sprockets connected to the lawn mower engine with the bike chains. The training wheels were attached to the either side as take off and landing stabilizers. The Soaring Sam wing was glued to the back of the sissy bar. The two kites were nailed to the side safety rails, above the two Cox airplane engines that would blow air against them and provide lift. The long kite tails, made out of rags, were rolled up and stuffed down the side between the seat and the wagon metal. The go-cart steering wheel was bolted above the front axle in the cockpit below the regular wagon handle.

No other kids in the history of the world had ever had a

better idea. And if they did, none of them had ever built it. We had. The Flyer was one of a kind. Nothing else like it existed, and there wasn't a plane in the world - none of the ones at Whitman airport and not even the big 747 - that could come close to flying the way The Flyer would.

The Flyer was gonna soar.

As we stood there admiring our work and all the intricate pieces that fit perfectly together, and the tiny adjustments we had made, and the way The Flyer now stood at a slight downward aerodynamic angle, it suddenly became completely clear to me why Bobby got that far away look in his eyes whenever he looked at it - even before we'd modified it. He had known something that I didn't all those times. He could see right through the metal of the wagon in wonder and imagine its true potential. It wasn't just the bright red paint, or the shiny white wheels, or the gloss black steering handle, or the way the logo was written on both sides so that it seemed like the words R-a-d-i-o F-l-y-e-r would race right off the metal if you didn't drive it fast like it wanted to be.

The fascination the wagon held for Bobby was what it represented.

It meant escape.

It meant freedom.

But more than anything, it meant the end of his nightmares about The King.

Who The King of Terrors couldn't see, who He couldn't get his hands on, who He couldn't stare into the soul of, he couldn't hurt. Ever.

Bobby was going away to far away places where the King could never hurt him again.

Forever.

That was what The Flyer was for, and that, pretty much, was "The Big Idea."

I went to the back fence and propped the loose boards of it open with a rake and a broom, then I went back and helped Bobby pull The Flyer through into the back field. I called Shane to come with us. He jumped through and I let the boards back down.

So far, so good.

We started across the field and kept bumping into bushes and general junk that was all over the place. We didn't use our flashlights because Chicky Erskine probably would've seen the light beams over her back fence and called the police. So it was hard moving through the dark, but we followed Shane - he had x-ray vision - and finally made it to the edge of San Fernando Road.

This part was going to be tricky. Even late at night like it was, there were still lots of cars traveling up and down the road. Somehow we needed to sneak The Flyer across four lanes, over and along the train tracks and across Osborne Blvd. to the airport, into and over the baseball diamond and finally wrench the plywood off the mine entrance and stash it inside. It occurred to us just then that none of this had occurred to us earlier.

First things first.

We took our coats off and draped them over The Flyer. They hid about all of it, but the Soaring Sam wing still stuck out on the sides. So I took off my sneakers and then my socks and put those over the wing tips. That did it. I put my sneakers back on and we waited for a clear shot across San Fernando Road.

The cars kept coming and coming. Then, way down the street we saw the traffic light turn red. The cars stopped coming from that direction.

This was our chance.

We pulled The Flyer out into the light of the street lamps and began to cross the asphalt. Just then, we heard it. WHONK! WHONK! A train. A long one with about four or five locomotives pulling it. It was coming from the left. The cars were still stopped from the right and we were in the middle of San Fernando Road. If we turned back we wouldn't get another chance to hide The Flyer. If we kept going we might get smashed by the train.

We pulled as we ran and got to the other curb. We didn't stop to lift The Flyer over it - there was no time - the train was closer now and if we stopped even for a second we wouldn't make it.

The light turned green and the cars started coming again from the right down San Fernando Road. In seconds we would be discovered.

The locomotive blew its horn again. The beam from its big headlight hit us like an interrogation lamp. Everybody could probably see us. We pulled harder. Ran faster.

Shane jumped across the tracks and the train was about 100 yards away. He barked back at us, telling us to hurry. We did.

Just as all of the cars drove by behind us... Just as the train got within 50 yards of us... Just as we thought The Big Idea was over and The Flyer was history...

We pulled as hard as we could...

And jumped...

And fell down in the gravel on the other side of the tracks.

The Flyer bounced over the first track, rolled about six inches, and the back wheels jammed against the tie.

In 20 yards the locomotive would smash The Flyer to scrap. It was a sitting duck. All of the work we'd done flashed in front of our eyes and Bobby screamed, "Mike! Get it!"

Suddenly, like God was helping us out, the wagon handle fell forward and banged against the track closest to me.

I grabbed it and pulled backwards like I was rowing a heavy boat.

The Flyer's back wheels released. It bucked over the tracks.

I did a backward somersault down the gravel and landed at Shane's paws.

The locomotive roared by shining its light ahead and everything went suddenly dark.

Under the train I could see all the cars that were stopped at the red light drive by on San Fernando Road. When the train passed, the street lights lit us up just enough for me to see The Flyer.

It was okay.

It had rolled across the tracks with no more than an inch to spare.

Bobby was hugging it.

I looked up to the sky for just a second and said, "Thanks."

We stuck close to the far side of the tracks as we continued on toward Osborne Blvd., where no one driving by on San Fernando Road could see us.

We crossed Osborne Blvd. no problem, because nobody ever drove on it at night.

We hurried through the entryway to the airport without incident and got to the far right edge of the baseball diamond. Nobody was there and the night-lights were turned off. That was good, but just to be safe we hugged the edge of the outfield all the way around to the boarded up mine entrance.

Bobby handed me The King's claw hammer and I wedged it between the plywood and the support beam. It only took one pry and the whole eight foot square sheet of it came falling back toward us. Bobby stepped out of the way and the board hit the ground with a sound like the mine was taking a deep breath. It didn't bang or nothing because the air softened its landing. It kicked up a lot of dust in the entrance and some of it got on Shane's nose. He sneezed and shook his head.

When the dust cleared all we could see was a pitch black void. But we could hear something. It was a strange sound, one that reminded us a little bit of the million frogs squeaking in the pipes at The 500. Then another sound started, like half pound butterflies all taking to the air at once.

Bobby and I squinted to see farther into the mine when suddenly a black cloud with little yellow dots in pairs all over it came rushing toward us. The squeaks got louder and shriller.

Bats!

I shoved Bobby to a nook on the left side of the mine entrance; I crammed myself into a cranny on the right. The cloud of bats flew by like a river of flappering black water, only the river of them was flowing up into the air instead of down along the ground. We waited for a long time and when the last bats finally trailed out they fluttered upward and disappeared against the night sky.

We got out our flashlights out and shined them into mine. We had expected to see something like the Diorama Grand Canyon along the Carolwood Pacific railroad at Disneyland. We'd expected Dinosaurs, wolves, coyotes, owls and eagles, phosphorescent pools of bubbling mineral juice, we thought there would be stalagmites and stalactites like in the caverns Mom took us to in New Mexico, and dirt walls dripping with water and mud and terrible dangers and natural wonders of all sorts. But as our flashlight beams cut into the mine, we saw none of those things. Just a long dark tunnel.

Except for the bats the mine shaft was okay, not even scary at all. Shane went in and checked it out. After a minute he barked and it echoed back to us so we knew it was safe.

We grabbed The Flyer and pulled it inside. It left wheel tracks in the dirt. We took it back as far as we dared until the tunnel split into two different passageways. Bobby shined his flashlight down the left tunnel and I pointed mine into the right one. Those tunnels sloped downward and disappeared after only a few yards. We had gone in far enough. We put The Flyer against the wall to the left just around the corner, where it would be hidden from anyone looking in from the entrance.

We started back out - passing beneath the old support timbers, and walked over the half buried ore cart tracks, by some old tools and buckets left behind by the Miners who'd worked in the mine a thousand years ago - and wondered why we'd never thought about exploring the mine before. It was the best place for an expedition, much better than our regular places, and our imaginations ran wild thinking up what might be farther down in the heart of the place.

"We should do an expedition in here sometime." I said to Bobby as we neared the entrance.

Mike, Bobby, Mom and our Little Sister. Carlsbad Caverns. 1972.

"Yeah, there's probably treasure and stuff way back in there." Bobby agreed.

Outside, we checked for spies and there were none.

Bobby grabbed the back edge of the plywood board and pushed it up. It fell back into place against the frame of the entrance. I nailed it back on tight. All the nails went back into the same holes they'd come out of, so no one would ever know it had been disturbed. Bobby found a dead tree branch nearby and starting at the bottom edge of the plywood, he swept the dirt backwards to the grass of the baseball diamond's outfield, erasing the wheel tracks left by The Flyer. It was a good thing he did it, because I hadn't thought of it.

Just as we were about to head back to the house, Bobby stopped and turned back to the mine. "Wait a second." He said.

"What?"

"How're the bats gonna get back in?" He asked.

"I dunno."

"We can't lock 'em out, that's their home." This hadn't occurred to me, but it was true, we'd just kicked about a million bats out of their house and then slammed the door closed behind them.

"How'd they ever get out before?" I asked.

"Maybe they never did, maybe they were trapped in there." Bobby figured.

"Yeah, probably. Maybe they ain't coming back neither. Maybe we did them a big favor and set them all free." This sounded good to me, and to Bobby too.

"I'll bet they're glad to be out of there." He said.

Just then one of the bats we had let out passed over our heads and its wings made a flootery sound in the air. We both waved to it and - at the same time - said, "You're welcome."

As we walked back across Osborne Blvd. to the railroad tracks along San Fernando Road, Bobby asked me something.

"Hey, Mike?"

"What?"

"You think those bats had a Big Idea too?"

"You mean like someday getting out of the mine and flying away?" I asked.

"Yeah."

"Sure, they probably got monsters in there too." I said, and we both believed it.

When we got home, Mom and our little sister were asleep. Everything was quiet like it had been for the last three weeks. We brought Shane in with us so he could sleep in our room. The King never let him in the house, so it was a treat for him. We got into our beds and each gave Shane one of our pillows. As usual, Bobby fell asleep before I did. I laid there staring up at the ceiling waiting for the Sandman, who I'd come to believe either didn't like me or just kept forgetting to knock me out too. So while I waited for him I remembered the double pinkie promise I'd made to Bobby and decided to run through the whole plan in my head to check for any possible thing we may have forgotten to do.

The Flyer was safe at the mine. We had all the other stuff for The Big Idea stashed under our dirty clothes in our closet. Friday after school we would get the donuts and postcards.

Saturday we would go to the Panorama Cinema, see Sinbad and be back in plenty of time to go through the loose boards in the fence, across the back field, along the railroad tracks, over the baseball diamond, get The Flyer from the mine, and pull it up the hill to The Wishing Spot above the airport long before The King suspected a thing.

We would wait until just before we left for the mine on Saturday to write the note for Mom explaining The Big Idea. That way it wouldn't be hanging around the house long enough for The King to discover it and stop us. Mom would probably be really worried. But we reasoned, that as always, she would understand.

Eventually, the Sandman remembered about me and I fell asleep. The Big One from Geronimo Bill's Buffalo Farm visited me again that night.

This time he came all the way into the room and spent the night watching over Bobby.

He didn't say anything, but I know he was there, and I know that it was real because it was the only night in the entire time we were kids after The King had become our new dad that Bobby slept through the night.

He didn't have a single nightmare.

By the time the sun came up, the Buffalo was gone and the wall and window in our room was back where it belonged.

That night, I was the one who had the nightmares.

I dreamt that someone was trying to break into the house by banging on the front door.

The Big One. Guardian Angel. Our room. 1973.

8

OFFICER CHRISTOPHER

"My son calls another man Daddy."
- Hank Williams

I woke up scared. It was already light outside and I looked at my watch and Mickey said it was 8:30 a.m. Mom and The King had already left for work and we were late for school. Then I realized I hadn't been dreaming at all. Someone was knocking on the front door. I woke Bobby up and we put our clothes on real fast.

We went to the front door and whoever was there started knocking harder. I peeked under the window shade to see who it was. Standing in our front yard were Chad and Ferdie and their mom, and just arriving near the curb on their bikes were big and little Raymond and the Hernandez brothers. On their way to school they had seen who was knocking at the door and stopped because their morbid hackles were up. I had to look up at an angle to see who exactly was at the door, because whoever it was was standing too close to it. All I could see was a shiny badge.

It was a policeman.

Chad and Ferdie's mom had really called them and they really were at our front door.

"It's the cops!" As I said it Bobby turned around and headed for the back door.

"Where you goin'?!" I said.

"To the clubhouse, they're gonna find The Flyer-" He cut himself off in mid-sentence, "-oh, I forgot, we hid it! Ha!" Bobby smiled.

"But if they look in the clubhouse and nothing's in there then they're gonna wanna know what was in there and where it is now." I told him.

We heard the policeman's muffled voice say, "Open up boys, I saw you at the window. I know you're in there." He knocked again, harder.

"What're we gonna do?!" Bobby asked.

"We can't let 'em look in the clubhouse 'cause if they see it ain't there, they're all gonna go looking for it." I said. We called Shane and we went out back to the clubhouse without answering the front door.

Once at the door to the clubhouse we could see around the left side of the yard through the chain link fence into the street.

Big Raymond saw us first.

"There they are! In the backyard!" He yelled to the officer who was still around front where we couldn't see him.

All of them; the Hernandez brothers, big and little Raymond, and Chad and Ferdie came around to the side fence and stared in at us like we were monkeys in a zoo. They were all holding their school books loosely, like throwing-bricks. Chad and Ferdie's mom waddled her way to the front of the crowd. They'd all rushed up to the fence and then slowed down like people do when they pass an accident on the freeway. The looks on their faces changed from curious to like the looks on the faces of the lions in the movie Born Free when they all get together to kill an antelope for dinner.

Behind the crowd the officer walked up.

A tiny wave of relief washed over us when we saw who it was.

It was Officer Christopher.

We already knew him and he knew us. Recognizing his face made us feel a little better when all that was staring back at us from the fence was a ocean of hate-faces. He knew Bobby and me because he was the one that usually came over when the loud things would start happening after The King had drained some of the blue and white cans in the garage.

He didn't look too mad, just bothered that he had to come over and look into the lying story that Chad and Ferdie's mom had told about us. But still, he was a policeman and she was a citizen, a fat one, but a citizen, and he had to serve and protect her too. As Officer Christopher hopped the fence and walked over to us we kept thinking that the only thing she really needed to be protected from was the bucket of chocolates she kept by her television chair.

Shane was sitting on the back porch; Officer Christopher didn't see him as he approached us. When he got within ten feet of us Shane came over and stood between Bobby and me and him. As soon as Officer Christopher saw Shane, he stopped. Shane didn't growl but he didn't take his eyes off Officer Christopher either.

"Does he bite?" Officer Christopher asked.

"Only bad guys." I told him.

"You sure?" Officer Christopher was looking at Shane and Shane was looking back.

"Yep." I told him again.

Bobby was standing closer to the clubhouse door than I was. He looked more scared than I did, so even though he was talking to both of us, Officer Christopher looked mostly at me.

"Boys," he spoke quietly so the mob at the fence couldn't hear, "the lady from across the street says you have some stolen stuff in your clubhouse -"

"- No we don't." I told him before he could finish.

"Well, she said -" Officer Christopher tried to go on.

"- She's lying." I said and could see her straining to hear what we were saying.

"Mike, it's not just her. All them other kids out there say so too. You telling me they're all lying just to get you and your brother in trouble?" It was a good question, but I had a better answer.

"No," I told him, "they're saying it because they don't like us." Officer Christopher squeezed his eyebrows together like he didn't understand. It was the truth, I said it like it was the truth and after a minute his face relaxed because he realized that I wasn't making it up. He took his hat off and wiped his forehead with his sleeve because, even that early in the morning, it was getting warm outside.

"Can I just peek inside?" He asked.

I shook my head and Bobby said, "No."

"Guys, I gotta look in there just to make sure. If there's nothing in there you have nothing to worry about."

"There ain't nothing in there." I told him.

"We're not lying, they are." Bobby added.

Shane was still sitting between us and him.

Officer Christopher folded his arms.

"Okay, I'll make you guys a deal. You let me look in the clubhouse and even if there is something in there, I won't tell anybody, not even them." He pointed over his shoulder to the mob at the fence.

I shook my head, because even though that was a pretty good deal Officer Christopher had offered us, we still couldn't let him look in the clubhouse.

Officer Christopher looked at us with his head tilted to one side like a curious dog. We looked back at him about the same way. After a minute he stepped forward.

"I'm sorry boys, I just have to." He said as he reached for the clubhouse doorknob.

When he reached out for it, Bobby stepped forward and bit him on the hand.

"Ah! Sweet Mother of ouch - !" Officer Christopher stepped back and shook his hand in the air until the teeth dents in his palm disappeared. His eyebrows squeezed together again, but this time he looked mad.

We were really scared, and even though Officer Christopher had maybe two hundred collective pounds on us, Bobby stepped up beside me and we stood our ground together knowing that if we had to we would even try and beat him up to keep him from looking inside.

We must have looked honest or maybe just different than other kids, because all of the sudden he didn't look mad anymore; he looked as if he could actually see the tiny storms of desperation that hung over our heads. I'm sure he felt that sad feeling you get when you pity someone so much you want to cry.

It was very quiet for a moment and the crowd at the fence was clutching the chain link, and looked like Romans in an old movie about to turn their thumbs down at the people they'd thrown to the Lions.

Shane walked away and went and sat over on the back porch. So we knew Officer Christopher was okay.

He got down on one knee and said, "I got a couple of boys at home about your ages. Maybe when your dad comes home I'll talk to him about letting you two come along on a fishing trip with us."

Although we never said it to each other, it was at that moment that we both had the same feeling - the one that gave us the worse ache in our stomachs we ever had. It made us cry right in front of him. It made a certain memory - that Bobby and me shared - race back up into the television parts of our brains where we could both get a good look at it in living color. The suddenness of it made us turn and look at each other, because although the memory itself was scary enough, it had, until that moment, been totally forgotten.

When we were still living in the apartment in Los Angeles, above the Aunt that we didn't know we had, I'd said something that got us in a lot of trouble.

Our Aunt had a husband, and they had a son who was our cousin. He was older than we were, so naturally we thought he was a big deal and we believed everything he said. We'd asked him once if his Dad ever hit him for doing stupid things like getting a report card that didn't have enough A's on it, or putting too much milk on his cereal. He'd said sure but that his Dad didn't hit too hard so it was no big deal.

An idea occurred to both Bobby and me when we heard the "didn't hit too hard" part. I was the one who approached The King with the certain plan we came up with. What I said didn't get us in trouble right away, it took a long time and resurfaced once after we'd moved into the house, when The King had drained about a whole case of the blue and white cans.

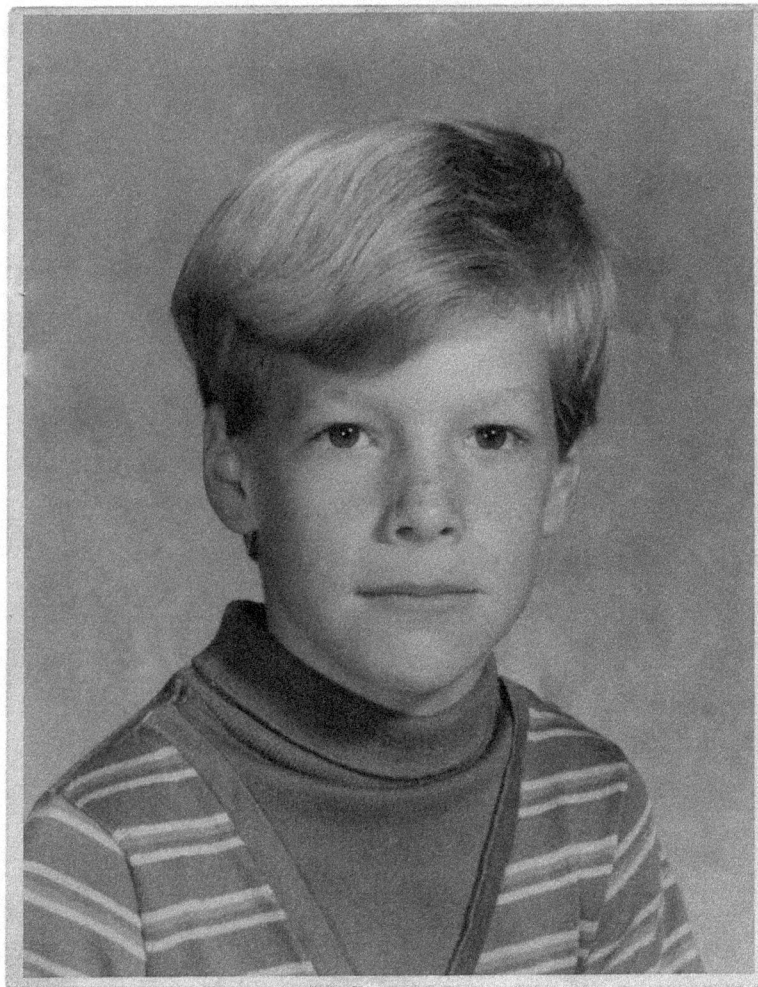

Mike, 4th grade class picture.
Montgolfier Elementary School. 1973.

After the cans were all empty, The King had called a meeting like he usually did at those moments. In that family conference The King turned to me and slurred, "Hey, you remember a long time ago, when you said that you wished that Frank was your Dad, because he didn't hit as hard as I do?"

He was almost right when He brought it up. The idea I had asked him about was a mutually beneficial arrangement, the innocent practicality of which He construed as malicious disrespect after a bout with the cans. The plan had involved Bobby and me moving into our Aunt's house so that The King wouldn't have to be bothered hitting us anymore, and we, when we did get hit, wouldn't get hit by Him. It had all sounded perfectly reasonable to us, but for some reason The King got mad.

Right after The King asked if I remembered saying what I'd said, I told him, "No..." because it was the first thing that made its way from my brain to my mouth. Apparently that had been the wrong answer, because that was the time I got punched and Bobby got his broken ribs.

When this all came rushing back to haunt us, we got our first taste of the terrors of deja vu.

Standing there, crying in front of Officer Christopher, we had heard him say something entirely different than asking us if we wanted to go fishing. We reckoned he'd said, "Why don't you guys come and live with me?"

That's why the memory came back and why the feeling of it made us at once terrified and happy. When Officer Christopher said what he'd said, Bobby and me wished he was our Dad.

Our sobs were the choked kind where you have to gulp in air between cries. Happy and Scared were having a war in our throats, and Scared was winning. We really wished that Officer Christopher or someone like him was our Dad. We really knew that if The King ever found out we'd made that wish, (and we knew he would because he could see what we thought) then something more awful than any monster we could conjure up would happen to us.

The crowd at the fence started snickering; they mistook our sobs for the "in trouble" kind.

Somehow, probably because he knew our short family history from having come over so many times before, Officer Christopher fathomed our problem. He may not have known exactly why we couldn't let anyone look inside the clubhouse, but at that moment, he knew that we hadn't done anything illegal and that whatever was in there (or not) was ours and not someone else's that we'd stolen.

"Alright, listen," he whispered, to be absolutely sure the crowd couldn't hear, "this is what we'll do. You guys stand aside and act like you're letting me look inside the clubhouse, and I'll fake like I'm peeking inside, but I'll have my eyes closed and I won't really look in." He motioned over his shoulder with his thumb again. "They'll think I did and I'll tell them there's nothing in there."

Bobby and I thought about it.

"Okay," Bobby finally said, "but no peeking. Pinkie promise." He held up his little finger to Officer Christopher, who, after a second, figured out what Bobby was doing and then locked pinkies.

"I promise." Officer Christopher swore.

We moved aside and Officer Christopher stood up and brushed himself off with his cap. He acted real official stepping up to the clubhouse door. Right when he grabbed the handle to open it, Chad and Ferdie's mom yelled at us, "Ah ha! Now you're gonna get it! You good for nothing thieving little brats!"

Officer Christopher turned his head slightly toward Bobby and winked at him. Then he closed his eyes just like he promised and opened the clubhouse door only a couple inches; so that no one else could see inside. He ducked his head in and held it there for a couple seconds. His eyes were still closed, I saw them. He closed the door and turned back around toward the crowd at the fence and hooked his thumbs in the front of his gear belt.

"I think you bunch owe these boys a big apology." He said to them.

Bobby and I wiped our eyes and were able to stop crying because for a second we figured our worries about The Flyer were over and that we had been proven innocent in the eyes of our accusers.

We looked over to the fence where everyone was still standing and staring. Their faces changed from mean-with-hate to angry-with-disappointment because a grownup had proved them all wrong. Our feeling of relief was short lived because mobs stick together until their lives are threatened, and theirs weren't. Bobby and I were still guilty and they wouldn't believe Officer Christopher's verdict anymore than they believed anything we said. Instead of admitting the truth when they heard it from a grownup, from a policeman, they just hated us even more.

The truth of the whole thing was lost to the Mob's embarrassment instinct. They had accused us of something bad and in the time it had taken the story to grow out of proportion enough for Chad and Ferdie to risk being branded tattle-tales by snitching to their mom, they had all come to believe it as the truth. In their eyes Bobby and me were guilty never to be proven innocent.

Officer Christopher approached the crowd and after exchanging a few words with them, in which it was obvious he was sticking up for us (we knew because when they started yelling after him, he loudly told them all to leave), the Hernandez brothers and big Raymond called him names and wandered away.

As they went, each of them looked back at least once and eyed Bobby and me with looks that meant, *"Just you wait."*

Before he hopped the fence and went back to the station, Officer Christopher told us that if anybody ever tried to look in the clubhouse, all we had to do was call him and he would stop them.

We told him, "Thank you."

Just before he left, I asked him to, "Please not ask our dad about going fishing with you, if you wouldn't mind not to, please?"

Officer Christopher was a great man because he understood exactly what I meant.

The King was due back the next day, Friday. If we could get through that day without anybody telling on us, without The King somehow finding out that the police had been over and that we'd been accused of stealing, and that we had used his tools, then maybe... just maybe, we'd make it to Saturday and be able to execute The Big Idea.

We stood near the clubhouse for a long time not talking, just waiting to see if any of the Telfair Ave. death squad was coming back for revenge.

Nobody came back.

We sat with Shane on the back porch and thought about The Flyer. It was still safe, that much we knew, but we also knew that because of what had just transpired the neighborhood goons would be trying to think of where we had stashed it. It might take a while, but sooner or later they would guess it was hidden in the mine shaft. We hoped it would be later, or at least after Saturday.

We asked Shane what he thought about our options considering the new development.

He told us that we had better stick to our original plan and just pretend nothing had happened so as not to raise suspicion; besides, he said, "You still have to get the postcards and donuts."

Normally Bobby and me and Shane all understood each other without having to say anything. But this time we talked to him and he talked back. He only spoke when the subject was really important, and only to us, otherwise he just barked.

Bobby and I agreed with him. There was nothing better we could do than what we were already doing - keeping the secret until launch time.

We felt better knowing that Shane concurred with our plan.

Through the entire construction phase of The Radio Flyer, Shane had watched over and protected us but he had remained silent. He had never told us what he thought about The Big Idea so we didn't know whether he approved or not. We reckoned he thought it was an okay plan, but that he just didn't have anything important to say about it.

That morning he told us that he thought The Big Idea was good, and that he too couldn't see any other way out for Bobby.

But as he talked we could tell something was really worrying Shane.

"Shane, whatsa matter?" I asked him.

"Nothing."

"You sound worried about something." I said.

"Nothing, Mike, really." He even sounded worried when

he said that.

"Is it about The Big Idea? Do you know something we don't?" Bobby fretted.

Shane tilted his head to one side and got that curious dog look on his face, like he didn't understand the question.

"Don't gimme that Shane, you understand what I said." Bobby said.

Mike, 11 and Bobby, 9. The Flyer completed.
Days before flight-night. 1973.

Shane thought a minute and we figured he was gonna stop talking right in the middle of a conversation like he usually did. But he went on, "No, Bobby, your Big Idea is fine. You'll be safe and The Flyer will fly. It's just..." Shane tilted his head the other way, towards me. "Mike, when is He due home?"

"Tomorrow. While we're at school probably," I answered, "Why?"

"Something will happen then." He said.

Bobby and I looked at each other for answers, and since we had none, we looked back at Shane.

"What?" We both asked.

"Something that I dreamt of." Shane said.

"What? Come on Shane, what?" Now he was worrying us.

Shane stood up and walked a few steps away then turned back to face us.

"I cannot say. Know that I love you both very much. Never forget that. Now, go, you are both late for school."

He was right about both things; first, that he loved us as much as we loved him, and second, that Bobby and me had lost track of the time. According to Mickey we were now an hour late for Montgolfier Elementary.

Shane moved away further into the backyard and lay down concealed from view behind the redwood cupboards beside the cinderblock barbecue. We went and collected our books and lunches and went back out back to see if Shane was okay. We were still worried about him.

"Shane..." I called for him but he didn't come. Bobby and I went around behind the barbecue and he was still there.

"Shane, if you'd tell us whatsa matter -"

But Shane barked, cutting Bobby's question short.

We knew then that he was all done talking.

He had nothing more to say.

9

SHANE

"As you love me, Buck. As you love me..."
- Jack London, The Call of the Wild

After three weeks of waiting and wondering whether The Big Idea would be discovered; whether we would be jailed or grounded for the rest of our lives, or killed, Friday, the day before the launch finally arrived. We had worked out every detail of the plan and constructed The Radio Flyer to withstand the rigors of the rough takeoff Bobby was bound to encounter down the hill from The Wishing Spot to the mine entrance ramp. Except for the episode with the crowd the day before, everything felt like it was going to work out.

But flight night countdown wasn't slated until the next day, Saturday, and we still had one problem to avert if we could. The King.

He was due back that day and if we could get past Friday without Him suspecting even the tiniest part of The Big Idea, then Bobby would be home free until Saturday.

And then he would be gone.

That morning Bobby and me woke up early for school and ate breakfast while Mom got ready for work. She'd made us oatmeal which we scooped out of the big pot on the stove - the same pot we had made the anti-monster goop in. We had milk and Karo syrup with it and what we couldn't finish we gave to Shane under the table; he loved oatmeal more than dog food.

Like the day before, he wasn't talking.

After Mom got her waitress uniform on, she changed our little sister and put her back in her playpen. She went into the kitchen to make her a bottle. As she heated it up on the stove she told us what we already knew, that He would be back that day, probably arriving home while we were at school.

As Mom came out of the kitchen she stopped and looked over at us with one eyebrow up and one down.

"Guys... Where's your oatmeal?" She asked. Under the table, Shane wasn't exactly being quiet about licking the bowls.

"He likes it Mom, 'specially the karo syrup." Bobby told her honestly.

Mom smiled, but the smile faded away as quickly as it came. She seemed to sense something, more about Bobby than me, and she sat down with us for a minute.

"What happened yesterday, guys?" She asked in a way that meant she already knew.

"Nothing." Bobby was looking down at the table when he said it.

"Some kids wanted to get in the clubhouse and we wouldn't let them, so Officer Christopher made them go away. That's all." I told her the truth because we never lied to Mom.

Mom looked back and forth between us trying to read our minds, which sometimes she could. Usually she let us tell her what was on them so we didn't feel like we were keeping anything from her.

"I know you guys have been spending a lot of time in the clubhouse the last few weeks. And I know you've been building something out there." Mom saw the dread come over us and then went on, "Don't worry, I never peeked. I don't know what it is. I know you guys wouldn't do anything you weren't supposed to, but please, whatever it is, can you tell me if it's going to upset Him?"

I thought about that one for a second. "No. It won't."

"Promise?" She asked.

"Yeah, we promise. It's not even gonna be around long

enough for Him to find about it. Don't worry Mom."
Though I knew she would because she always worried
about us being home while He was and she wasn't.

"Okay." She said, smiling at us again. "You're gonna be
late for school." As Mom got up to give our little sister her
bottle, a feeling of grave realization gripped Bobby,
although he probably felt it as aching pre-homesickness, and
he shouted, "Mom?!"

She turned back around startled, then concerned.
"What, Bobby?"

Bobby struggled for a moment; it was then that I knew
why he had shouted. It had occurred to him all at once; we
were leaving for school, Mom was going to work, she
would probably be back late and we would already be
asleep; Saturday we would be at the Panorama Cinema all
day and then up at The Wishing Spot before she got home
that night. Bobby had suddenly realized right at that
moment that it might be the last time he ever saw his
mother.

"I love you, Mom." Was all he said. And as it would
turn out later, that was the last thing he ever said to her. I
figured that was a pretty good thing to say for a last thing.

Bobby and me got to school at 8:00 a.m. All during that
day we didn't say anything to anybody in case we goofed
and mentioned The Flyer.

At lunch we sat by ourselves on the playground and ate
baloney and cheese on Wonder Bread in silence. We knew

He'd be back before we got home and even though He never so much as even looked at the clubhouse all that summer, we shared a common feeling of dread that this day out of all days in the history of the world, He would dig up or manufacture some reason to go out back and look inside it. Of course He wouldn't find The Flyer because it wasn't there, but something told us, gnawed at us because of what Shane had said, that somehow, some way, by way of some piece of evidence we'd left behind, that The King would discover The Big Idea.

It wouldn't take much, just a missed screw or a wood chip, and The King would put it all together. Just like Sherlock Holmes, He would construct the entire plot in his head right down to the last detail. He had that ability, to deduce things, as sure as He was able to read our minds. He was a lot of things, but stupid wasn't one of them.

If He found The Flyer we expected to at least be maimed, if not dead for sure. But the chances were slim on that; He'd never even been over to the airport and so didn't know about the mine shaft. But it wasn't so much The Flyer that we were worrying over. It was something else that we could not put into words. A feeling of dread, a sinking ache in our guts told us we should cut school at lunch and run all the way home as fast as we could. We had no idea why, the feeling was just there in our stomachs. It was exactly like the feeling you get standing on a boulevard corner trying to gauge traffic. There's a unceasing stream of cars. You wait for the precise moment to cross. You make the decision and start out into the street. You look back, and in the split second you'd looked away the cars are right on top of you. You bolt back the way you came just in time to avoid being killed.

We fought that feeling all through school that day.

When the 3 o'clock school bell rang, we still wanted to run the whole two miles back to our street. But we had to get the donuts and postcards.

We took the bus to the Five & Dime store in San Fernando and got four postcards; good ones with desert and beach pictures, and one with Disneyland on it. We took the bus back to the corner of Osborne Blvd. and Laurel Canyon Blvd. and got a dozen glazed donuts at the Yum-Yum's. We hurried back to the corner and waited for the bus. When it came we realized that the box of donuts in our hands represented the very last of the twenty two dollars we had made collecting pop bottles during all those weeks.

We would have to walk home.

It was about the same distance as walking home from Montgolfier Elementary, so it wasn't going to take long, maybe forty five minutes, but as the bus pulled away from the curb and finally out of view, the forty five minutes seemed like forty five years and made the dread-filled ache in our stomachs kick into full gear.

Something was wrong.

Something worse than we could imagine.

We started home.

I waited for Bobby to catch up at each corner, so that slowed us down a little. But not as much as the feeling in our guts which got worse the closer we got to home.

By the time we were four blocks away our progress had slowed to a crawl; just putting one foot in front of the other became more difficult than it had been in any running-away-from-a-monster-dream either of us had ever dreamt.

We were out of breath as we came around the last corner and could see the house at the end of the block.

We walked that last piece and stopped when we came to the front yard. We could see around the side of the house into the backyard and because the cardboard was still up in the windows of the clubhouse, we knew He hadn't looked inside and discovered any tiny bit of evidence to punish us for.

The relief was so weighty that we had to sit down on the curb and wait for our hearts to stop thumping like locomotives. Ten years passed in the next five minutes before we got up and walked toward the house.

Although we were sure that The Flyer remained undetected, something else was wrong. Every step up the cement walkway brought the bad feeling in our guts closer to the surface of our skins, right up where you can really feel your hairs crawl.

It was about 90 degrees that day but we got cold with every one of the ten concrete squares we stepped on as we approached the front porch, until by the time we got to the front door we were shivering.

The door was unlocked so He was home, that much we already knew - his van was in the driveway. But He wasn't in the house, so that meant he must be... in the garage.

As it turned out mom's prayer to Saint Ann worked for around six hours and thirty five minutes. We quickly calculated that that had been how long He had been home before He went into the garage with the Jazz and cans.

We could hear it and we could smell it.

Our little sister had been left alone in her playpen and she was bawling her eyes out. She had her bottle, her diapers were dry, there was nothing wrong with her but she was crying. By the time Bobby and me got to the back door, my fingers were so cold I could hardly wrap them around the doorknob to open it and go out back.

The first thing we checked, of course, was the clubhouse. It was locked. Neither The King nor anyone else had tried to get into it. But we already knew that, so for some reason -

the ache in our guts was now hot like coal fire

- we were stalling. We stood facing the clubhouse for a minute wracking our brains and kicking at the dirt trying to figure out what was wrong. Everything looked normal. Even the Jazz coming from the garage was normal. Our little sister was bawling, but that was normal, except that she didn't have anything to bawl about.

What the was going on?

It wasn't until we turned around and faced the entire backyard that the horror finally rose up to suffocate us like a dirt pillow.

As we looked across the grass toward the garage, the whole backyard seemed to rise from the ground and smash down on us like a giant lawn wave. For several minutes we were disoriented in the violent turbulence of the swirling grass and dirt. Then like a riptide, the whole lawn receded back down to earth and settled into its original, and tortured state.

The backyard was torn to shreds.

Shane?

Big patches of grass were ripped away and flung all over the place.

Shane?!

There were long clawed furrows and deep pits near the back fence where someone -

SHANE?!?

- had tried to dig out. The redwood cabinets beside the cinderblock barbecue were smashed to bits. It looked like someone had driven a bulldozer into the backyard and spun roosters for vicious fun. But fun had as much to do with what we were looking at as aerodynamics did with making The Flyer fly.

There were only two times in our lives when Bobby and me were so scared that we actually feared we would die of fright. The last time, although bad, couldn't hold a candle to what we were seeing.

The first time was when Bobby and I had seen the grossest thing we ever saw. It was after an expedition to the buffalo-frog drainage pipe at The 500. We had made a good collection of frogs that day; so many that they kept hopping out of the bucket on our way to the Frog Lady's house.

She came to the door with a cigarette butt in her mouth and glasses on her face with lenses so thick they made her eyes look like big, squashy, rotten plums.

"Oh, sweet Mary! Those are juicy amphibs!" She'd apparently never seen any bison-frogs before and the sight of them made her kind of chirp like a bird. She was so impressed with our catch that instead of the regular dollar fifty, she gave us two bucks for the bucket. Then she told us to dump them in her pond, which we did.

We squeezed through the moldy wooden fence under a willow tree so tall, wide and droopy that it never let any light into her house. We dropped the frogs into the pond and they made plopping sounds as the hit the muddy water. Only thing was, there weren't any other frogs in the pond. There should've been; Bobby and I had sold her at least twelve buckets-full in the past. But none of them remained. Those that we'd just dumped in crawled up and clung to the edge of the pond, half in and half out of the water. As we stood there looking around for the lost frogs, her back door banged open behind us and we spun around.

"Frogs in the pond?!" She hacked, lighting a new cigarette with the butt of the one in her mouth.

Bobby and I nodded.

"Okay then, git!" She squawked and we obeyed. We ran back around the side of her house, through the moldy wooden fence and onto the dirt road out front. We were about to leave when two fishing gaffs of curiosity hooked our collars and yanked us back toward the Frog Lady's house.

We had a suspicion about her. About what she did with the frogs.

We felt like maybe we shouldn't be collecting and selling them to her anymore, we didn't know why exactly but the gut feeling was strong enough to make us risk sneaking up to her kitchen window and peek in.

We crept up the left side of her house along a brick wall and squish-stepped over a million-year-old pile of fungusy leaves. The whole path was like walking on a mildewed trampoline. We stooped down under her kitchen window and Bobby almost jumped out of his skin.

"Ahhh! -" I slapped my hand over his mouth to shut him up. He pointed down near his feet.

There, uncovered by the disturbance we'd made in the rotting leaves, was a potato bug the size of a baseball. I couldn't scream because the Frog Lady would've heard it; I couldn't take my hand off Bobby's mouth because he would've hollered like a steam whistle and got us busted. So with heebie-jeebies running up my spine I turned the frog bucket upside down and covered the potato bug with it. The thing almost didn't fit underneath, its legs were stretched out and wriggling, trying to right itself. Why potato bugs even have legs is a total mystery - every time we ever found one it was always on its back trying to flip over, so what was the use of them having legs? And this one was a mutant, it even banged against the inside of the bucket trying to get out. I sat on the pail and took my hand away from Bobby's mouth.

"You jerk!" He shout-whispered, "That thing coulda bit me!"

"Well it didn't, so shut up." My heebie-jeebies turned into woollies sitting on the bucket; I could feel the russet-killer pounding on the metal of it.

Then, slower than molasses in Alaska, Bobby and me stretched up to get a look inside the Frog Lady's kitchen. We were plastered so close to the side of her house by fright, that we got red burns on our noses as they slid up the stucco toward her window.

We were totally unprepared for what we were about to witness.

Her window shade was pulled down and since it was yellowed with spoiled grease it was hard to see inside. We managed to peer through either side of it where it had curled in; like the Frog Lady's fingernails, just enough for us to see the frogs.

Live frogs.

Dead frogs.

The kitchen was a frogoture-chamber.

The Frog Lady was a frogaholic.

She was a froggydermist.

Everyone of the little green croakers we had sold her she'd either eaten (there were half-eaten frog carcasses all over the dinner plates she never washed) or made into little stuffed pets. There were hundreds of them; on shelves; on the sink counter; on the fridge. Everywhere!

Two pots on the stove were at full boil. Beside the stove, in a twenty gallon glass aquarium, were the ones we'd just sold her. They were still alive and clawing at the slick glass sides trying to get out.   The Frog Lady appeared in the kitchen from somewhere down a long dark hallway. She opened a drawer, reached in and pulled out the longest, sharpest, biggest butcher knife we'd ever seen.

I glanced at Bobby, his eyes were big as scooter pies. He was breathing faster. He was gonna scream at any second. The Frog Lady dropped her cigarette on the kitchen floor among a trillion others and stepped on it. She lifted the lid off one of the boiling pots and set it aside.

She bent over and looked into the glass aquarium.

She grinned.

She reached into the grappling mass of bison-frogs. Frogs don't talk, but we heard screams. Tiny squeaking screams.

She grabbed the biggest one in the tank and held it up examining it. It was a three pounder, no doubt. She kissed it on the belly but it didn't turn into a prince. She held it over the boiling pot and Bobby screamed, "Nooo!!!"

She turned toward the kitchen window, knife in one hand, Buffalo-frog in the other. Suddenly, the window shade furled up and we were totally exposed to what happened next.

She smiled at us like a witch and did a turn-a-round, fall-away jump-shot with the frog.

The green croaker flipped through the air exactly like the rubber ones at carnivals do when you try and launch then onto plastic lily pads with a catapult n' hammer.

The Buffalo-frog arched and splashed down. He landed in a full bellyflop in the center of the boiling pot of water. He almost made it back out but the Frog Lady had only filled the pot up to a certain point, so no matter how hard he kicked, he couldn't grab the rim of the pot and pull himself out.

We watched in stark raving terror as the bison-frog grappled for the rim... boiling... cooking... dying, turning from green to pink... to bright red. And then, he was still. He bobbed and floated and twirled and turned over on the turbulent surface of the bubbling water. Bobby, screamed, "Nooo!!!" again.

The Frog Lady laughed so hard she started hacking and

chucked up something yellow and chunky that she
thwapped into the sink from ten feet like an old water-rocket
toy.

We couldn't take anymore. We ran. And ran. And ran.
All the way to the Jessup dairy, where we bought two
twelve packs of wax bottle cokes and slugged them fast to
calm our nerves.

We never, ever collected or sold frogs to the Frog Lady
again.

We were more scared then than any other time in the
whole time we were kids. More scared that is, except for the
moment we turned around and saw the backyard all tore up
the way it was.

Something worse than watching live frogs boil had
happened while we were at school. We stood there near the
clubhouse feeling all of a sudden sick, and when we looked

at our hands, all twenty fingers were blue.

We followed the tracks in the dirt and grass to the north side of the house where the garbage cans were. When we turned the corner I screamed and Bobby threw up.

We saw the reason our sister was still crying, she must have heard the whole thing while nobody from the neighborhood had apparently done anything to stop it. The reason we'd been stalling -

we had known, the gut feeling had told us

- Shane was dead.

The heavy tow chain he had been beaten to death with was in the dirt beside him. Even though he was limp and motionless, he was still tied to the fence post so he couldn't escape.

The back door to the garage crashed open and The King stumbled out. There were terrific bite marks on his legs and his left arm was caked with blood. Shane had gone down fighting.

The King spoke in a very even, normal voice.

"Don't ever use my tools again. Ya hear me?" He shut the door. We had heard Him.

Although He had no idea what we had built with them, He had found out we had used His tools. And since He couldn't wait until we got home from school to whip us, He had killed Shane instead. He knew exactly what made us live and breath.

We knew right then that we couldn't wait until

Saturday; Bobby had to go that night.

We buried Shane near the sunflowers in the field behind the fence and made a cross with our Genuine American Indian rubber tipped, bamboo spears.

Later, I told Mom that, "He just ran away."

Burying Shane in the back field with a prayer. 1973.

10

THE FLIGHT

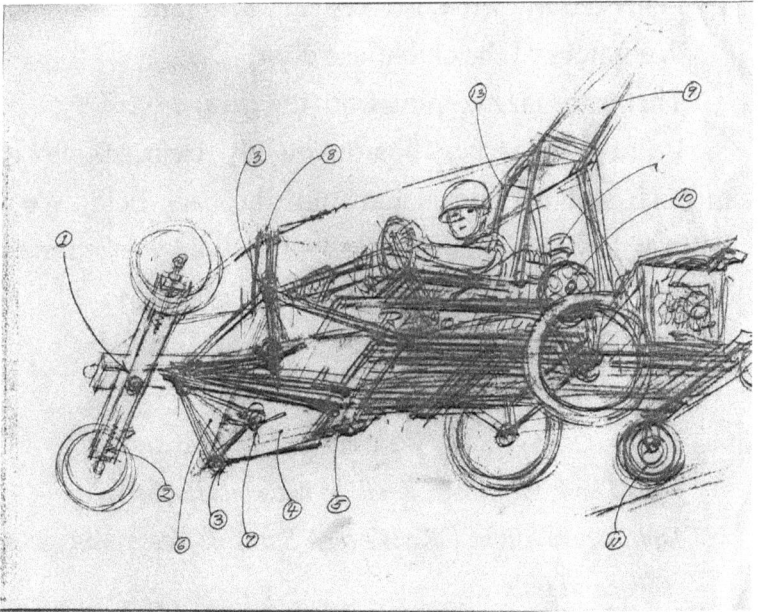

"You can fly."
- Peter Pan

First thing we did when it got dark was make sure our little sister was fed and then asleep. Then I wrote the note to Mom explaining The Big Idea and put it in an envelope and put that in the crib with our sister.

Bobby got out The Big Idea list and checked it over.

I got Samson and put him in a box with a towel. We

took him and all of the other important stuff on The Big Idea list that wasn't already loaded on The Flyer, and went and locked ourselves in the clubhouse to have a pre-flight supplies check.

Everything was ready.

I checked my wrist, Mickey said 8:45 p.m.

We unlocked the clubhouse door.

There was jazz coming from the garage.

I lifted the fence boards quietly clear. Bobby went through and I followed him into the back field. We were halfway to San Fernando Road when Bobby asked me what I had written in the note to Mom, so I told him:

Mom,

Bobby has to go now. We went to The Wishing Spot
with The Radio Flyer. I will be back but Bobby wont.
Dont worry hill be OK. We took Samsin, pleese dont get mad.
-Mike and Bobby.

We only made one stop, at the gas station on the corner of Osborne Blvd. and San Fernando Road to fill up an empty peanut butter jar with gas for the lawn mower engine. We traded the man seven pop bottles for 35 cents worth of Super.

We crossed to the railroad tracks and followed them to the entrance of the airport. We could hear that there were still planes taking off at 9:15 p.m. when we got to the baseball diamond. Not many though so we figured Bobby would get a good takeoff spot. We made it across the left field and got to the mine entrance at the bottom of the big hill by 9:20 p.m.

Bobby took off his soapbox backpack and got the hammer out of it. We had kept it because we were going to need it; that it was missing was how The King knew we had used his tools. He gave it to me and I wedged it between the plywood and the support beam. One crank and the plywood fell back opening the mine. No bats came out this time. They hadn't come back after we'd let them out a few days ago. They were, we guessed, finally free.

We checked the area.

No one was around.

We went inside to get The Flyer.

Shining our flashlights ahead of us, we found The Flyer exactly as we'd left it. The mine had turned out to be the perfect hiding place.

Instead of loading it when we got to The Wishing Spot, we did it right there so everything would be ready when we got to the top of the hill.

We tied Samson to the back of the wagon and loaded the lunch box, the Highlights, the pin-hole camera, the Disneyland map, and postcards and donuts underneath the special new cockpit we'd built. Bobby put on his warm, long cowboy duster jacket and Davy Crocket coon skin cap and then the motorcycle helmet over that. Then he put my lucky rabbit's foot in his pocket.

We checked over every part of The Flyer.

Everything was tight and tuned and polished and perfect.

The Flyer was ready.

We punched holes in the bottoms of the Yuban coffee cans and knotted the ends of one mile of string inside them. Bobby would take one end while I held the other; we would be able to talk for about a minute after he was airborne.

As Bobby pushed, I pulled The Flyer by a rope over my shoulders, it was the harder job, but it was my cross to bear. We pulled it out of the mine tunnel and into the night. We let it sit for a minute while we swept all the dirt and rocks off the top of the mine shaft entrance so The Flyer would make a clean launch.

I was just about to nail the plywood back in place to be absolutely sure nobody could track us up to The Wishing Spot when we heard a shrill screech!

In the half second it took us to look back, we already knew it was The King's van skidding into the baseball diamond parking lot. We knew He had found the note we'd left for Mom and was coming to kill us.

We heard it again, SCREECH!

Searching into the darkened parking lot, however, we didn't see any headlights.

We looked back around toward The Wishing Spot and

there, perched on the phone pole, were the mother and father Red Tail Hawks. It was as if they were telling us to hurry to the top before He really did show up.

We let the plywood lay where it was and started up the hill.

Since The Flyer weighed more than we had expected and we had to clear the bigger rocks and sticks from the takeoff path, we didn't get to the top until 9:55 p.m. In five minutes Mom would get home and find the note.

We turned The Flyer around and pointed it down the hill and chocked the back wheels with rocks. Then we sat down and rested. We hadn't said much to each other since we'd left the clubhouse, but as we sat there looking all the way across the whole San Fernando Valley to the Chatsworth mountains that night, Bobby made the last wish he would ever make at The Wishing Spot. A wish that would never come true.

"I wish Shane was here." He said.

The Chatsworth mountains were the mountains we hoped Bobby would be flying over in about ten minutes. We sat and stared into the night for longer than we should've and were only brought back into the real life moment - the launch of The Flyer - by the tiny sounds of Dave Brubeck jamming in our garage six blocks away.

The Wishing Spot. Pre-flight check. 9:55 p.m. Flight-night. 1973.

We counted three planes lined up at the end of the runway and decided that Bobby would go after the third one.

When the first one took off Bobby got into The Flyer's cockpit.

When the second one took off we both took our ends of the Yuban coffee can telephone and I got ready to kick the wheel chocks loose.

For some reason the third plane didn't move. It just sat there waiting, making us nervous because it was after 10 o'clock now and Mom was probably home and she had probably already found the note and was just now probably calling the police because she was worried.

"What're you cryin' for?" I asked Bobby.

"I ain't cryin'. You're cryin'. What're you cryin' for?" He answered.

"I ain't, you are." I told him.

"No I ain't, you are."

We would usually go on like that for ten minutes at a stretch, but we both knew we didn't have any more time. Even though that third plane hadn't taken off yet Bobby had to go. And he had to go now.

"Oh, I almost forgot, here," I handed him the four postage stamps. "For when you send me the postcards."

When Mickey hit 10:15 p.m. and the third plane still hadn't taken off, suddenly another loud, angry screech echoed up from the valley of death. And this time it wasn't the Red Tail Hawks.

It was The King.

Down in the baseball diamond parking lot, He ran his van through the backstop and fell out onto the infield screaming at the top of his lungs. We couldn't tell what He was saying but it was loud and angry and we understood exactly what He meant.

He turned toward the big hill and we could see he was clutching a blue and white can. He looked up and somehow saw us at The Wishing Spot.

He ran staggering toward the hill and started scrambling up it yowling whatever He was yowling; which, as he got closer, we finally heard as a promise to kill us, over and over.

We knew he was serious.

We could see it in his other hand.

He was carrying ol' trusty. Somehow he had found where we had hidden the long electric cord from the Corningware coffee pot. It was frayed and had jagged bits of copper wire sticking through the insulation from having been used so many times in a manner for which it was never designed, but nonetheless painfully effective.

As The King cleared the top of the mine shaft entrance and struggled to get a foothold in the loose dirt, three more cars raced into the parking lot.

Mom was in one of them.

Chad and Ferdie and their Mother in another.

And Officer Christopher in his patrol car.

But that wasn't all; both Raymond's and the Hernandez brothers rode over on their bikes. They altogether ran into the middle of the baseball diamond and stared up at me and Bobby and The Flyer.

Mom screamed for us to come down.

Chad and Ferdie and their Mother stood there and pointed.

Little Raymond just stared.

Big Raymond and the Hernandez brothers threw rocks at us.

The King kept climbing. He was halfway up now.

"Get a chopper over here!" We heard Officer Christopher bark into his police radio.

I raced through the pre-flight check list and Bobby mirrored my words with the actions:

"Fuel level?" I asked.

"Topped off. Check." Bobby answered.

"Flaps?"

"Check."

"Rudder?"

"Check."

"Supplies?"

"Donuts. Extra clothes. Thermos of milk. Samson food. Postcards. Check."

"Map?"

"Check."

"Ailerons?"

"What?"

"The up and down things. On the kite wings."

Bobby actuated the ailerons. "Up and down things. Working. Check." He confirmed.

At 10:20 p.m. the third plane finally started down the runway. I took a half step backward to kick the rocks loose from The Flyer's wheels. Just as my foot got halfway through the kick the sun suddenly came out and blinded us. It was a police helicopter search light.

"Just stay where you are! Don't move! Freeze or we'll fire!" The sound blared out of the speaker above us and echoed down the small canyons between the hills below us.

Bobby and I froze; we didn't want to be shot. It wasn't until I felt a hand around my ankle that I realized they were talking to The King.

He had made it all the way up the hill to The Wishing Spot, and the police in the helicopter could see him.

I jerked my foot loose and He swung the full length of ol' trusty at me.

It swooshed like a bull whip over my head as I ducked.

He fell forward under the force of His swing and hit the dirt. His head bounced off the rock under The Flyer's right rear wheel knocking it free. The remaining chock was not enough to hold it back.

The Flyer crept forward leaving wheel tracks to the edge of the big hill. Bobby and I looked at each other one last time.

He grabbed the go-cart steering wheel and hung on.

Just before The Flyer crested the edge, I reached out and grabbed the lawn mower start cord. I didn't even have to yank on it, The Flyer went forward and it unwound in my hand. The engine started and the rear wheels dug in. I clamped the Yuban can to my ear to listen and leaned over the edge to watch.

As Bobby picked up speed everyone below on the baseball field turned to stone. It was as if the whole world had suddenly slowed on its axis under the enormity of what was now happening: a nine year-old boy in a Spanky MacFarlane jalopy was racing down a ten percent grade toward a twenty foot ramp around thirty miles an hour. And gaining speed.

He was, at that moment, in all of their eyes, no more alive than Fisher was.

I could see Mom turn away and hide her eyes against Officer Christopher who couldn't take his eyes off Bobby and The Flyer. I caught a momentary glimpse of his face in the wavering beam of the searchlight from high above and he was, at that instant, as a model American father, utterly astonished by the length to which we had gone to get Bobby out.

Halfway down the hill Bobby hit about forty miles an hour. I had calculated that he would need to be going fifty miles an hour for The Flyer to launch over the runway fence, and from there the Soaring Sam wing and the kites would take over.

When Bobby got within thirty feet of the mine shaft ramp, The King staggered to his feet. He looked over the edge just in time to see Bobby compress down in the stroller seat, against the sissy bar, under tremendous G-force as The Flyer hit the ramp.

The front wheels cleared the air.

I felt the world stop dead in space, un-turning for a fraction of a second and everyone on the baseball diamond looked like they were under a strobe light as they turned back to flesh and bone and covered their eyes with their hands and their heads with their arms.

The Flyer was airborne.

And it was climbing.

It gained considerable altitude and then...

It apexed.

My heart stopped and I lost my breath like someone had just kicked me in the solar plexus.

The Flyer was falling.

It didn't work.

The lawn mower engine whined and the rear wheels spun like crazy with nothing to bite into.

Bobby screamed into the Yuban can, "Mike! I'm falling! Help me!" It was as if Fisher himself were screaming forward from the past, falling from the sky with nothing to hold on to, his belief having left him, his life about to end.

The Flyer was nose diving.

In seventy five feet, Bobby would become nothing more than a memory.

The Big idea was a failure.

The Flyer was a waste.

I had killed my own brother.

Just then, not a second before and not a second after, but right exactly at that specific most important moment of our lives, probably because Saint Ann answered another prayer, I suddenly remembered. I wedged my Yuban coffee can over my mouth and the string started to go tight - we didn't quite have a mile of it only about seven hundred feet - and yelled into it with all the pure faith I could possibly muster.

The coffee can amplified my voice into a big, tin roar, "The Cox engines! Start the Cox engin--"

That was all I could get out before the string snapped. But Bobby had heard me.

The Flyer was forty feet from impact when he reached back with both hands and grabbed both of the Cox model airplane engine start cords.

He yanked forward.

They started.

The paper kites braced out against the air suddenly pushed up into them. Their long rag-tails unfurled, snapping out behind The Flyer.

When falling from the sky and just ten feet from the pitcher's mound... Just as Mom fainted... Just as the third plane lifted off over the runway...

The Flyer pulled up.

It didn't fly like a plane though, it sort of floated like a blimp.

It went up about three hundred feet and eased over the runway fence, across the airport, over San Fernando Road, past the police station, gained another hundred feet or so and vanished into the darkness above our house.

When the world started spinning again, everyone on the baseball field was staring into the sky with their mouths wide open and their necks craned back.

I watched as all of the remaining legends and myths about Fisher's fearless feat swirled up out of their throats, collected in a ghostly vapor above their heads, and completely vanished from the face of earth.

I ran down from The Wishing Spot yelling as loud as I could yell: "Robert Radio Flyer is The King of Pacoima!"

Bobby. His escape vehicle waiting to be assembled.
Christmas morning. 1969.

11

LONG DISTANCE

GREETINGS FROM

KILL DEVIL HILLS

*"If dreams were lightning, and thunder were desire
This old house woulda burnt down a long time ago."*
- John Prine, Angels From Montgomery

Two people who were there that night for the flight of the Radio Flyer knew what happened to Bobby. Another two did not. It had to be that way for Bobby's own protection and so that the operational secrets of The Flyer would never be revealed. Eventually though, when the King was no longer a threat, I told the remaining witness everything. Everyone else who was at the baseball diamond that night never believed what they saw.

In the few years before I turned 13 years-old, Mom never stopped asking me. I had tried explaining to her what had happened without breaking my promise to the other keeper of Bobby's secret about a hundred times, but being a grownup she could not recapture the frame of mind needed to really understand.

Nine years went by before she finally accepted that Bobby wasn't coming back. In those nine years she never once said a word to The King.

When The King eventually lost his battle with alcohol, it was time for me to tell her the truth. It was long after the day I turned 13 years-old and had almost lost all knowledge of the seven great abilities and fascinations having become a necessary, albeit unwilling, member of the grownup world. But I had been in contact with Bobby's caretakers and they told me that often, very often, it was as if Bobby simply wasn't there. In those times I was the only one who knew where he was. I had known exactly where he was because for the first two years he was gone, and before I had lost all knowledge of the seven great abilities and fascinations I ran home after school and grabbed the mail before anybody got home.

So I got the postcards.

The Wright Flyer. First successful powered flight.
Kill Devil Hills, Kitty Hawk, North Carolina. 1903

The first was postmarked Wilkes Barre, Pennsylvania, a small town about 200 miles outside Harrisburg. Our home town. I got the postcard about the same time I heard a news report concerning two small boys (brothers of nine and eleven) who claimed they were rescued from drowning in Harvey's Lake by a very small UFO that looked like a red wagon.

The second was postmarked Kitty Hawk, North Carolina. Three days after I received this one, the main headline on one of the national tabloids caught my attention while I waited in line at a Dale's Jr. Mart. The story hailed from a small gas station about 11 miles from the exact spot where Orville and Wilbur first flew. The 75 year-old station owner claimed that late one night, as he was closing up shop and on his way down the road to The Wright Flight Inn for a night cap, a boy in a coon skin cap pulled up to the Ethyl pump in, what he termed: "The damndest flyer I ever saw."

He claimed to have traded the boy 40 cents worth of Ethyl for six large pop bottles. Then, he swore (to his eternal discredit) that the boy and his vehicle puttered away down the road, bounced along the divider line for a few hundred feet, and finally lifted smoothly into the air in exactly the same way he, as a boy, had seen Orville Wright do it in The Wright Flyer, at Kill Devil Hill in Kitty Hawk in 1903.

The third one was postmarked Cocoa Beach, Florida just south of the Kennedy Space Center. The date on the postmark was April 12th, 1976, about five years before the launch of the Space Shuttle Columbia, which would've put the project's development in the designing phase at that time.

Although the reports were sketchy at best, and the incident was resolutely cloaked in a classic blanket of military denial, and eventually vanished from public consciousness, it is believed that the designers of the shuttle gathered together late one night on the outskirts of the famed launch pad and met with someone; a small boy, and something; a strange machine.

They were said to have analyzed a device known to the boy who allowed them to look it over, only as, The Flyer. When after exhaustive analysis the designers were completely baffled as to how The Flyer flew, the boy is said to have left them a list of materials from which they gratefully cribbed invaluable advice, suggestions and technical data. Although the list was lost and little, if anything, is known about its contents, one puzzling bit of information remains. A retired Aeronautical engineer (who wished to remain anonymous) who claims to have been at the secret meeting that night on the Cape, said that the title on the paper of infamous list was: "The Big Idea."

The Wright Brothers. Glider test. On a wing and a prayer.
Kill Devil Hills, Kitty Hawk, North Carolina. 1902.

The fourth one, the last one I received, was postmarked Main Street U.S.A., Disneyland, Ca.

I went to college after that and rented a small apartment

near the campus where I wrote my way through the tuition and struggled for a long time wondering if I had done the right thing on Bobby's behalf. But that worry, like my lingering deja vu about the seven great abilities and fascinations, never slipped far enough into the past to become, like the legend of Fisher, no more than a cloudy memory that slowly broke apart and floated away. I never forgot. I was lucky. I think.

The worry finally vanished one day while I was visiting Mom and her phone rang. It was a long distance call from an Air Force base in Altus, Oklahoma. A place, as it turns out, very close to where there was once a place called The Geronimo Bill Buffalo Farm.

It took the operator a good while to connect the call through. When the connection was finally made, it was full of static and crackles - as if from far in the past. Mom handed me the phone and said, "Mike, it's a bad connection, I can't hear the voice. Who is this?"

I took the receiver. "Hello?" I said.

"Hey, Mike... Someone wants to say hello to you."

"Michael, who is it?" Mom asked.

"It's Samson." I told her. When she didn't seem to understand, I said, "Tortoises, especially the hearty desert variety I read somewhere once, Mom, because they carry their homes with them wherever they go, live a long, long time."

The heavy weight of years of her own worry lifted from

her shoulders. I'm sure it did, because right then, for the first time in her life Mom was happy.

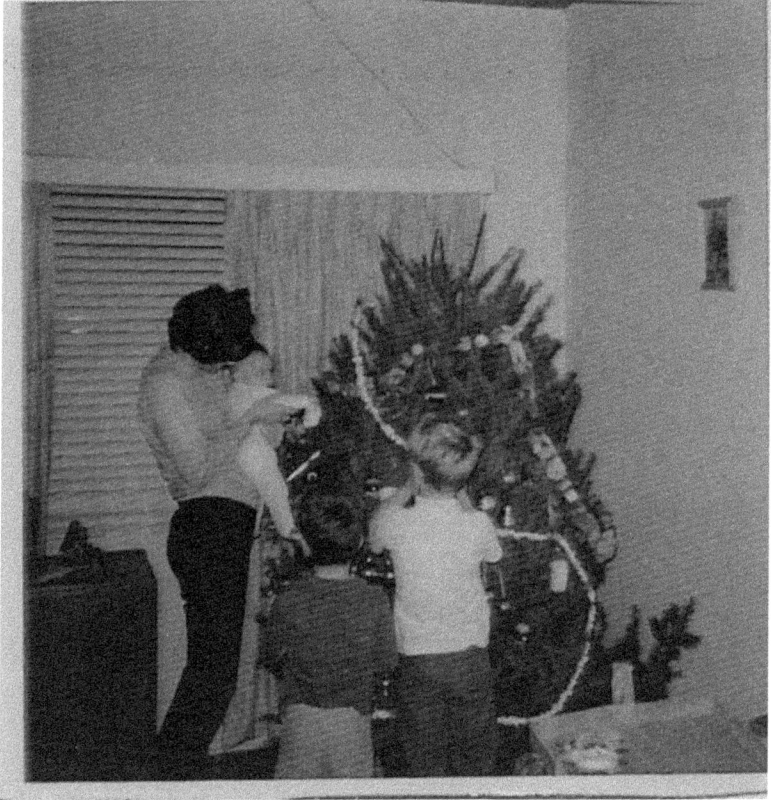

Mike, Bobby, our Little Sister and Mom.
One blessed night of no worries. Christmas Eve. 1969.

EPILOGUE

*"The streets looked small, of course.
The streets that we have only seen as children
always do I believe when we go back to them"*
- Charles Dickens, David Copperfield

*"On these magic shores children at play are for ever beaching
their coracles. We too have been there; we can still hear the
sound of the surf, though we shall land no more."*
- J.M. Barrie, Peter Pan

"No person ever died that had a family."
- Ray Bradbury, Dandelion Wine

One summer many years later, when I had two boys of my own, we took a long road trip. It was a cross country journey, and I made sure to revisit - in reverse - all the great places that Mom and Bobby and me had seen more than thirty years earlier on our trip from east to west.

Most of the places from decades before were gone. Geronimo Bill's Buffalo Farm was then just vast flat land dotted with oil rigs painted like giant grasshoppers endlessly rocking up and down. The small town, though, was still there. There were apartment buildings this time, but the town still had a shop-lined street with a swirling red and white barber's pole; an ice cream parlor with a spotless chrome soda fountain; a helpful hardware store; a sweet smelling tobacco shop whose wooden Indian that used to stand guard outside was gone; a post office with brass clerk's cages and a new young Post Master who smiled at my sons when they bought stamps for the postcards they sent their mother from the road.

I had timed it so that my boys could see the annual 4th of July VFW parade I had watched with such wide eyes when I was a kid. The veterans were younger this time, having fought a different, and different kind of war.

We did, however, detour from the original route; going to and exploring the following four places before we reached our final destination...

... Our trip began in Anahiem, California at Disneyland U.S.A. Somewhere east of Oklahoma we turned east-southeast to the Kennedy Space Center at Cape Canaveral, Florida, then north to Kill Devil Hills at Kitty Hawk, North

Carolina, then continued north to Wilkes Barre, Pennsylvania ending at Harvey's Lake. From there we drove down to our final destination: The Smithsonian Institute's National Aerospace Museum - the world's most important repository for the preeminent artifacts of flight.

Located on the National Mall in Washington, D.C. it is the place where almost all of the world's most famous and historically important aircraft are displayed.

With my sons on either side of me, holding each by a hand, we walked together through the entrance doors and were met by a friend of mine from my college days - who had, in the intervening years, become the curator for the entire museum. Some months earlier I had shipped him a large crate that contained something I thought he might be interested in putting on display in the museum. After seeing what was inside the the crate, he had immediately agreed. I had timed our trip to coincide with the three days before the display went public.

As we followed my friend through the museum, my sons were enthralled, necks craned back looking up at all of the ceiling-suspended greatest flying machines that had ever flown: including Charles Lindbergh's Spirit of St. Louis, the Apollo 11 command module, the Bell X-1 (the first plane to break the speed of sound), the X-15 and most especially the machine that started it all: The Wright Flyer. All of these aircraft were held aloft by almost imperceptibley thin stainless steel wires.

"Dad," my older son asked, "Those wires are really small. How can they hold up all that weight?"

"Because," I answered, "those wires are not really just one wire. Those are small cables made up of many even smaller, thinner wires - wound around each other, holding each other tight - that together make them very, very strong. Together, each of those small wires is able to shoulder much more weight because they have the other wires to rely on."

Just before we arrived at the cordoned area, behind which was the new display not yet open to the public, I looked back and saw a tall, handsome man in a United States Air Force Officer's uniform enter the museum. If one had knowledge of the meaning of the insignia adorning the chest of his uniform jacket, which I did, one would have immediately identified him as a Lieutenant, and a Test Pilot. We nodded to each other and my younger son asked, "Daddy, who is that?"

"Someone you're going to meet in a minute. He's your uncle." I answered.

My curator friend stopped at expansive drapes which, like grand theater curtains, separated the new, unseen display from the rest of the museum. He smiled and stepped away, and I lead my sons behind the red velvet curtains into a vast hall, directly in the center of which was the National Aerospace Museum's newest, astounding artifact; its most unique and unimaginable display.

As my sons approached the new display, an old

apophthegm from the days before the Wright Brothers first flew at Kitty Hawk came to mind, "If God had meant man to fly he would have given him wings." Seeing The Flyer again after so many years, I couldn't help but smile at the decidedly positive flip-side of that very negative adage which had meant so much for Bobby decades ago - like a tossed coin that never fell to the ground, but just kept tumbling skyward.

There was, in a word, nothing in this world to account for what we were looking at just then. Or more to the point, nothing at all to account for what this machine was doing. And therefore what it was clearly capable of. Or, again once more, what it was clearly capable of doing without the slightest regard for the "Forces That Affect Flight."

As they circled in astonishment, my sons, 8 and 10 years-old at the time, and so still solidly in command of the Seven Great Abilities and Fascinations that leant them understanding of what was before their eyes, they nonetheless sought some small clarification. It was just then that they asked the questions I had been waiting all their young lives for them to ask me.

"But, Dad..." my younger boy said, "there's no wires. What's holding it up in the air?"

"Hope, Orville" I answered.

"Yeah, but what makes it fly?" My older son asked.

"Dreams, Wilbur."

The Flyer. On display. Smithsonian National Air and Space Museum. Present Day.

THE END.

ABOUT THE AUTHOR

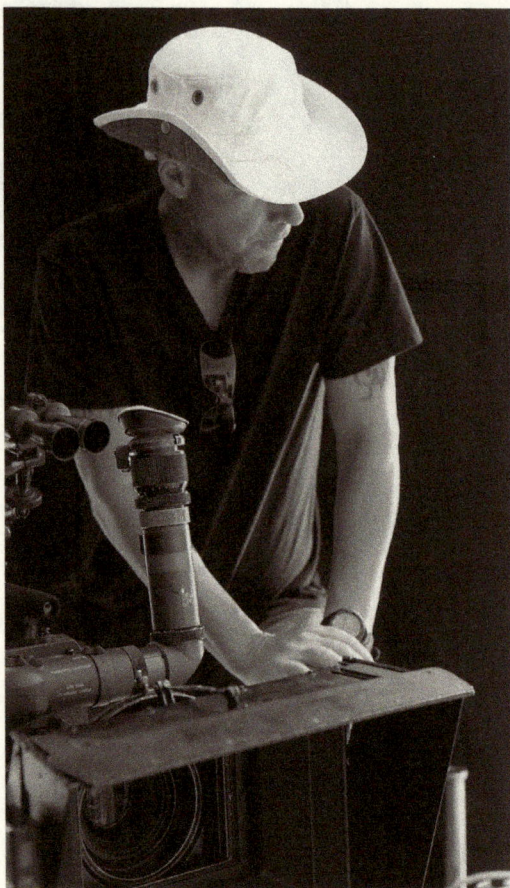

Photo by: Patti Arpaia http://www.pattiarpaia.com/

David Mickey Evans is an Author and motion picture Writer/Director.

Directly after college he became Hollywood's highest paid screenwriter, breaking records with the sale of his first two scripts, Radio Flyer and The Sandlot.

The Sandlot has been hailed as the greatest baseball movie ever made and the best summer movie of all time. Dialogue from The Sandlot is some of the most often quoted in movie history, including the classic line, "You're killin' me, Smalls!" and the unforgettable, "Heroes get remembered, but Legends never die."

Mr. Evans lives in Florida.

You can contact Mr. Evans at:

Twitter: @DMESandlot

Email: FlyingWagonBooks@gmail.com

Blog: http://davidmickeyevansblog.blogspot.com/

www.ingramcontent.com/pod-product-compliance
Lightning Source LLC
LaVergne TN
LVHW041216080426
835508LV00011B/972